Black Towns, Black Futures

Black Towns, Black Futures

The Enduring Allure of a Black Place in the American West

Karla Slocum

The University of North Carolina Press CHAPEL HILL

Publication of this book was supported in part by a generous gift from Florence and James Peacock.

The University of North Carolina Press has been a member of the Green Press Initiative since 2003.

Library of Congress Cataloging-in-Publication Data
Names: Slocum, Karla, 1963– author.
Title: Black towns, black futures : the enduring allure of a black place in the American West / Karla Slocum.
Description: Chapel Hill : University of North Carolina Press, [2019] | Includes bibliographical references and index.
Identifiers: LCCN 2019011078 | ISBN 9781469653969 (cloth : alk. paper) | ISBN 9781469653976 (pbk : alk. paper) | ISBN 9781469653983 (ebook)
Subjects: LCSH: African Americans—Oklahoma—History. | Cities and towns—Oklahoma—History. | Oklahoma—History.
Classification: LCC E185.93.04 S58 2019 | DDC 976.6/00496073—dc23 LC record available at https://lccn.loc.gov/2019011078

Cover illustration: Photo of U.S. flag by author.

Portions of chapter 2 were previously published in "Black Towns and the Civil War: Touring Battles of Race, Nation, and Place," *Souls: A Critical Journal of Black Politics, Culture, and Society* 19, no. 1 (2017): 59–74.

Contents

Preface ix
Acknowledgments xiii
A Note on Place Names xvii

Introduction 1

CHAPTER ONE
History Stories 19

CHAPTER TWO
The Case for America 40

CHAPTER THREE
Economic Futures 69

CHAPTER FOUR
Community of Blackness 106

CHAPTER FIVE
The Appeal of a Black Place 131

Epilogue 136

Notes 141
Glossary of Place Names 153
Bibliography 155
Index 167

Illustrations, Map, and Table

ILLUSTRATIONS

Oklahoma History Center's Black-town sign, **Tatums**, Oklahoma 20

Boley Town Council, circa 1907–1910 28

Former Black-town school 35

Reenactment of Honey Springs Battle 62

Pecan Street, **Boley**, Oklahoma 70

Closed Dollar Store, **Langston**, Oklahoma 74

Jess Dunn Correctional Center, **Taft**, Oklahoma 101

Boley Rodeo and Bar-B-Q Festival souvenir program 111

Pecan Street during **Boley** Rodeo and Bar-B-Q Parade 113

Black fraternal organization marching in **Boley** Rodeo
and Bar-B-Q Parade 116

Lowriders in **Boley** Rodeo and Bar-B-Q Parade 117

Lowriders in **Boley** Rodeo and Bar-B-Q Parade 118

Letchen Hill's grave at **Boley** Elementary School 135

MAP

Freeland and adjacent Black communities 91

TABLE

State prisons in Oklahoma's Black towns 99

Preface

In 1969, my grandfather died at the age of fifty-eight from a contaminated blood transfusion. I was a young child at the time and barely knew him. However, posthumously, he is the force behind this book. Mozell C. Hill, my grandfather, spent more than seven years researching and writing about Oklahoma's rural Black towns—the more than fifty post-Reconstruction-era communities for people of African descent—or what, in his day, were called "All-Negro Societies." I only came to know this and so many other things about him twenty years after his passing when my grandmother succumbed to cancer. In the spring of 1989, my aunts, mother, sister, and I were cleaning out my grandmother's Harlem apartment and, while going through books on her balcony bookshelves, I came across texts by Black artists and scholars that had belonged to my grandfather. A just-starting-out graduate student, I was immediately taken with the extent of the collection. Although I knew that my grandfather taught at a university when he died, it was on that balcony that I gained a fuller sense of his intellectual life, the writers and thinkers who influenced him and the works that were important to him. It was also on that balcony that I first learned that my grandparents lived in a Black town, **Langston**, Oklahoma, the same town that he wrote about in his dissertation and where he worked at the state's only historically Black university, Langston University. This "discovery" led me to start inquiring about my grandparents' and mother's life in Oklahoma, and my mother became my primary source of information. Once I started asking questions, she was happy to share the stories.

There are the stories, for instance, of her childhood days in **Langston**. She recalled an outdoorsy and playful life full of days catching snakes with her preadolescent friends. She also boasted of her exceptional academic experience. The classes in her Black-town school were mixed age—primary and secondary grades housed together in one school building, she recalled. She remained convinced that this was the reason she skipped two grades when the family moved to Chicago briefly in the late 1940s. "I was exposed to things that kids in grades ahead of me were learning," she said.

Outside of **Langston**, she remembered life as less familiar, even uncomfortable. In **Coyle**, the White town neighboring **Langston**, she recalled an air of hostility toward Blacks and how her family never went there. "Stay away from **Coyle**," she warned me, when I made my first trip to Oklahoma. She also described a trip that she took with her mother to **Guthrie**,[1] once the capital of Oklahoma and about fifteen miles from **Langston**. In her recollection, this was the first time that she had left **Langston**, around the age of four. In a **Guthrie** store, she spotted a blonde White girl and, grabbing a lock of the girl's hair, she said out loud to her mother, "Mommy, what's this?" She had never seen a White person before that trip, she told me as she was wrapping up the story.

Parts of my mother's stories resemble what elder residents in Black towns today will tell you about their childhood and community, past and present. They describe Black towns as bastions of freedom after encountering racism in the Jim Crow South. They recount experiencing community, comfort, easier living, and strength in Black towns. Outside the towns, they often describe danger, disorientation, and unease—in the past and sometimes even today.

In many ways, my grandfather's research reflects these same themes. In his dissertation, articles, and book,[2] he argued that Black towns were utopian in their outlook, mostly socially egalitarian, and economically advanced, with many active Black businesses. In many ways, he described them as committed to being "race communities"—that is, communities organized around and proud of their Black identity as well as supportive of other Blacks. Black-town residents, he showed us, were committed to keeping distance from Whites due to their experiences and recollections of horrific oppression in the South.

My grandfather came to his conclusions about Black towns in part from his brother, who moved to the Oklahoma Black town of **Boley** in the early twentieth century. According to my mother, her uncle extolled the virtues of the place to the rest of his family still living in the South and Midwest. However, my grandfather's graduate education also shaped his thoughts about Black towns. As a doctoral student at the University of Chicago in the early 1940s, he became a proponent of the theory known as symbolic interactionism, the idea that interactions between different groups of people (in the case of his study, between Blacks and Whites) were meaning-filled, subjective encounters that influence groups' identities and how they organize their individual communities.[3] My grandfather was interested in the social organization of Black towns. Yet, his focus was on whether the circumscribed nature of Black towners' interactions with Whites, as well as the priority that Black-town residents placed on interactions with Black community members, shaped how the town populace functioned and thought of itself. He found that Black-town youth demonstrated higher self-esteem than Black youth living in "mixed-race communities." He found that the towns were not very hierarchically organized, and so class divisions, although they existed, were not strong.[4] He found that Black towns had prominent successful businesses, which he attributed to Blacks banding together and wanting to support members of their community.[5] And while he seemed critical of the more "hard line" (or "Old Timer," as he called them) Black towners who advocated for zero interaction with Whites, to me he (and his sometimes coauthor, Thelma Perry Ackiss) comes across as sympathetic to those residents who did not support Blacks interacting socially with Whites but who did advocate for Blacks participating in business and politics with Whites.[6]

My ideas about Black towns have been influenced by my training in cultural anthropology (a cousin of my grandfather's brand of sociology) and also by my research, which has involved engaging regularly with Black-town residents and their communities. However, as was the case for my grandfather, my family ties and newfound family stories play a role in how I think about the towns. My mother's memories as well as my research constructing who my grandfather was as a Black-town scholar, Black-town resident and employee, and the brother of a Black-town pioneer have also shaped how I have come to understand and think about the communities' past and present.[7] Like many new Black-town residents and visitors, I represent the kind of curious seeker for whom memory and personal history play a part in the motivation both to connect with Black towns and to understand what Black towns are. At this intersection of subjective experience and empirical research, I offer my study of the broad appeal of twenty-first-century Black towns for those of us who, through a variety of reasons, have become investors in Black towns' stories and their possibilities.

Acknowledgments

In 2013, the mayor of **Langston**, Oklahoma, wrote to me to say he was anxiously waiting to read my book, and he asked that I please not forget him when it was finished. Dr. Hinds was a kind individual and Black-town champion. He was also a supporter of my research and inquired often how the writeup was coming along. It is hard to convey in words how much I regret that writing this book took so long and that he passed away before it finally materialized. I hope that he would be pleased with it.

I feel particularly indebted to so many people in Oklahoma like Dr. Hinds. To protect their anonymity, most of them will remain nameless. However, I want everyone I met in Oklahoma, especially residents of the Black towns, to know that I appreciate their generosity of time and reception of my research assistants and me. Black towns draw no shortage of interest from outsiders. Like many Black communities that have been frequently studied, I am sure that some Black towners experience what someone once described to me as "research fatigue." I am therefore grateful to those who allowed us into their homes, welcomed us to join their activities and attend their meetings, drove me around, invited me to their churches, and were open to me hanging out with them in so many ways.

I am also grateful to the people and organizations in Oklahoma that provided me with useful information or helped me set up an aspect of my research in their community or area of work. Thank you to the African American Resource Center at Rudisill Library, Guthrie Territorial Museum, Honey Springs Battlefield Park, Oklahoma Alliance for Geographic Education, the Oklahoma Council of Black Mayors (OCBM) — especially former Mayor Murrell, the Oklahoma Historical Society, Oklahoma Tourism and Recreation Department, Bruce Fisher, Ralph Jones, Larry O'Dell, Alicia Latimer, Oscar and Sharon Ray, Heather Seifert, and the late Cassandra Gaines and Lansing Lee. I feel grateful to all who, during my research, were mayors of Black towns. I did not meet all of them, but my work was influenced by their leadership, which I became aware of either by visiting the towns or attending OCBM meetings. Of those towns I visited, all mayors were also welcoming of me, and for that I extend my sincere appreciation.

I was helped by two dedicated research assistants, Suzette Chang and Sekou Clincy. Although both were new to the study and the kind of ethnographic research I was asking of them, they learned quickly and the project is all the better for their skilled involvement. For my project that was spread out over multiple communities and that I kept active sometimes when I was back in North Carolina, Sekou's and Suzette's assistance was valuable and critical.

I thank my editor at UNC Press, Lucas Church, who was critical in shepherding my manuscript through the production process and who has been supportive, thoughtful, and patient. Two anonymous reviewers also provided useful comments that, I believe, helped make parts of the manuscript stronger and sharper.

I was aided by several individuals who were then graduate students at the University of North Carolina. They conducted archival research and assisted with some images that appear in the book. Many of them jumped in on short notice and gave me timely, useful assistance. Thank you to Orisanmi Burton, Caela O'Connell, Taylor Livingston, Maggie Morgan-Smith, and Andrew Weeker. Thank you also to Deborah Mitchum, who was an excellent and careful transcriptionist of my many interviews.

Without funding, the scope of my research would not have been possible. I appreciate financial assistance from the following organizations: UNC's Center for the Study of the American South; UNC's Center for Urban and Regional Studies; the National Endowment for the Humanities; the National Science Foundation Cultural Anthropology Division; and the School for Advanced Research.

A number of colleagues and friends have also provided support by advising me on aspects of the project, offering suggestions or reading drafts of my work that became book chapters. Some of them served as formal consultants on the project. I thank them for their careful reads and friendship, both of which helped my process. They include: Anna Agbe Davies, Michelle Boyd, Kia Caldwell, William Darity Jr., Keith Clark, Kamela Heyward-Rotimi, Bayo Holsey, Laurie McIntosh, Brandi Summers, Tanya Shields, Karolyn Tyson, and Rachel Watkins. I also thank colleagues in UNC's Anthropology Department who have provided interest and encouragement as well as served as a sounding board for aspects of this project, particularly Florence Babb, Rudi Colloredo-Mansfeld, Arturo Escobar, Valerie Lambert, and Charles Price.

Additionally, during my fellowship at the School for Advanced Research (SAR), I benefitted from comments and support I received from my fellowship cohort, which doubled as a writing group, as well as from members of the SAR staff, who include: Alex Blanchette, Lisa Barrera, James Brooks, Tatiana Chudakova, Danika Medak-Saltzman, Elise Edwards, Margaret Pearce, and Ageeth Sluis. In addition, I tested out my ideas at various talks where audience members' comments were helpful for the final shaping of the book. Especially useful was input during talks at the University of Chicago Department of Anthropology; the University of California–Berkeley Department of Geography; the University of California–Los Angeles Ralph J. Bunche Center for African American Studies; UNC–Chapel Hill's Department of African, African American and Diaspora Studies; the 2016 Black Americas Network conference at the University of Bielefeld; and the University of Copenhagen's Rural Aspirations workshop in the Department of Food and Resource Economics. I am especially grateful for invitations to these talks from Sharad Chari, Jovan Lewis, Robin D. G. Kelley, Stephan Palmié, Mattias Borg Rasmussen, and Willie Raussert, as well as from graduate students at the University of Chicago. I also thank all of those staff members without whose administrative work to make my visits possible my project could not have advanced. At UNC-Chapel Hill, this includes especially Irina Olenicheva and Matt McAlister in the Anthropology Department as well as Linda Comer, Holly MacPherson, and Judith Bukenya at the Center for Urban and Regional Studies.

My final stretch writing this book was during the years when I was director of the Institute of African American Research (IAAR). While IAAR has no direct relationship to the project, I know that the unit's staff bore some of the brunt of my divided time and attention while I tried to write a book, teach classes, and run an institute. At IAAR, I especially appreciate the patience and support of Angela Hicks, Amatullah King, and Rosa Perelmuter.

In the course of doing the research for this book and writing it up, I became a parent, and my mother passed away. Both events challenged the time and energy that I could devote to getting to the home stretch. But the flip side is that my family helped carry me through. They were excited about a project that had something to do with our family history, and their encouragement every step of the way has been valued moral support. Some of them were "in the trenches" with me, helping me with aspects of the research, checking my referencing, and looking over my writing. For this, I have eternal gratitude to Alyce Hill, John Elsoffer, Edmund Newton, Riley Newton, Robbin Slocum, and Cheryl Slocum.

Above all, I must thank three people. First, my grandfather, Mozell C. Hill, whose pioneering, rare, and important work on Black towns, in the short span of his life, inspired me and sustained me. Suffice it to say that I have grown to know him better by researching Black towns and, after a fashion, retracing his steps. Second, my mother was also a critical catalyst for my research, particularly (and ironically) as the only living family member with recall about my extended family's days in Oklahoma. Our regular conversations comparing my experiences in Oklahoma with memories of her childhood in **Langston** were simply great; they became a valued dimension of how I came to make sense of Black-town life. As with Dr. Hinds, I regret that my mother cannot read the book that I always imagined I was writing, in part, for her. Lastly, it is for my son that I have the most gratitude. He has motivated me to finally finish the book not only so that I can give him more of my time that he has missed over the past few years. He also motivated me to get this story out because, ultimately, I want to show him how important it is for there to be places in the world that will affirm his worth.

A Note on Place Names

Throughout this book, I use a mixture of pseudonyms and actual place names to talk about Oklahoma Black towns. When I talk about events that are publicly known, I tend to use actual place names. When I talk about practices and events that are not public and were disclosed to me through my research, I use pseudonyms to provide anonymity and confidentiality to participants in my research. To differentiate the uses of actual names and pseudonyms, when I refer to Black towns by their actual names, the names are in bold type. When I refer to the Black towns by pseudonyms, the type is not in bold. See the glossary for a full listing of place names in this text.

Black Towns, Black Futures

Introduction

A Black El Dorado

My mother sometimes told a story about my great-uncle Letchen, who, sometime in the early 1900s, was making a decent living as a barber in a small Alabama town. That was a nice accomplishment for an African American in those times, my mother noted. One day, she said, a White barber moved into town and ran my uncle out of business in a very hostile way (the details of that hostility my mother did not share with me). Uncle Buddy, as he was affectionately known, was furious. He packed up his bags and headed to Oklahoma, where, he had heard, Black Americans were developing rural communities known as "all-Negro" towns. In these towns, Black people were thriving and living free from racism. It was like a Promised Land. And once he arrived in this Promised Land, my mother said, Uncle Buddy swore that he would never return to the Deep South. Why would he? Uncle Buddy—once a deposed Black business owner in the Jim Crow South—went on to become the mayor and superintendent of schools in **Boley**,[1] the largest Oklahoma All-Black Town (as the towns are now called). He became an exemplar of the Black-town success story: the African American who freed himself from racial hostility, became economically self-sufficient, and raised his social status by settling in a community of Black people committed to uplifting themselves. The way my mother told it, Uncle Buddy's story was about Blacks refusing racism during the Jim Crow era, attaining security, and gaining a chance at social mobility by relocating to a new place seemingly their own.

The especially intriguing part of Uncle Buddy's story is what feeds its denouement: the rise of a beleaguered and highly vulnerable person—a Black man—whose ascent is made possible by an ideal place that protected him from pernicious conditions that so many others like him were unable to avoid. The people in the place matter, but the place—the town on lands controlled by Blacks who achieved incredible things within those town borders—is the essential piece of the story of Uncle Buddy's rise. The Black town and what people organized within it enabled his ascent.

Important to this story is also the narrator, my mother, who recounts the events after having heard the story decades ago from her own parents. She did not tell me the story until I was an adult and had embarked on research about Black towns; it is possible that she might not have shared the story with me otherwise. However, once she did, she was passing on a stand-out family account about something that occurred close to a century ago. A story about a family member who surmounted a challenge and succeeded when he joined a Black community. It's an appealing story about an alluring place.

This book examines early twenty-first-century accounts and activities (specifically for the years 2004–2012) that mark Black towns as appealing places. Across the following pages, you will hear and see people narrate Black-town life and engage in Black towns in ways that identify the communities as places of attraction. Two features are especially important for the towns' appeal: their Black identity and their status as "historically significant." For other reasons, the towns' rural locations are also part of what makes the towns appealing. A range of people leverage, connect, and capitalize on these features in ways that prove materially beneficial to some and stimulate the memories, hopes, and aspirations of others. Through stories, events, and interactions, you will see how the towns get people remembering and thinking about greatness in Black life, how great Black life can be, and what Black life has contributed especially to America. The Black town—with its particular connotation as a race-specific and historically important small place—is a vehicle for remembering, explaining, and imagining exceptional qualities of Black life, especially Black-community life. However, you will also see people reconciling and sometimes lamenting the challenges of life in a small, rural Black place, while others see opportunity and take advantage of those challenges. You will see that not everyone agrees about Black towns; there are competing visions of the towns' contemporary value and uses. You will meet people like my mother who wanted to share a great story about a small, historic, rural place that, for her, marks our family—our extended family—as having had (and as *having*) a good Black life. And yet, you will also encounter nonresidents (some who are not Black), former residents, some Black residents, private investors, tour agency operators, and even officials of the state of Oklahoma who tell different stories that complicate the picture of a good Black-town life, all the while—I believe—showing that Black towns are an attraction.

Because Black American places are often obscured, you may not have heard of Black towns before reading this book. Black towns—as small, rural places known mostly for their past—are especially obscured. The little-known but conventional story of Black towns is one you will find in just a few history books, some museums (especially in Oklahoma), selected tourism materials (also in Oklahoma), and papers in scholarly journals, particularly those devoted to history. This (condensed) story goes like this: Following Emancipation, hundreds of towns were created across the United States for the settlement of Black Americans as a pathway to Black freedom.[2] Due to their material and social success, the towns bolstered Black Americans' status.[3] Oklahoma received the largest concentration of such towns, and Black-town settlement in the West reflected patterns of westward expansion and town settlement in nineteenth-century America.[4] Black Americans who forged Black towns in the West did so alongside White Americans who were also claiming land and forming settlements in the region.[5] However, the motivation to establish Black towns was racially specific and part of a larger national movement that spawned Black settlements in Kansas, Colorado, California, Iowa, and Illinois.[6] Whites were seizing a chance to acquire property, expand horizons, and enhance prosperity. Black Americans heading West were also seeking opportunities for gaining land and economic growth. However, there was a particular urgency to Blacks' movement, as they were often fleeing life-threatening racism. In this way, Blacks who ended up in Black towns were like so many other Blacks who left the South after Reconstruction, just before and especially during the Great Migration.[7]

Joining Blacks who came from the South to Oklahoma were groups known as Freedmen (the term is meant to encompass all genders), people of African descent formerly enslaved by Native Americans and already settled in the West.[8] With westward expansion, the 1887 Congressional act known as the Dawes Act broke up communal tribal land structures, allotting lands to individual tribal members. Although some tribes resisted inclusion of Freedmen on the tribal rolls for purposes of land allotment, in many cases Freedmen acquired up to 160 acres per individual.[9] In some instances, these lands became the basis of Black towns as Freedmen sold their allotted lands to profit-seeking White town speculators, who then resold parcels to migrating Blacks.[10] In other cases, Freedmen used the lands they acquired to form Black towns alongside African Americans coming from the South. Thus, at the same time that Whites were settling in large numbers in the rural West, two groups of African descendants in the United States were also forming and developing towns for their own settlement.[11] As has been the case with other interactions among different groups that make up the African diaspora,[12] relations between Freedmen and African Americans were not always harmonious, especially because the former considered the latter more accommodating of Whites. Freedmen feared that the arrival of Blacks from the South would shift the existing social order in which Freedmen had maintained some degree of distance from their former enslavers. Yet both groups sought freedom from hostility and established communities for that purpose.[13]

My grandfather, Mozell C. Hill, who studied Black towns, considered Black-town formation a utopian movement.[14] His work fit with that of other scholars who contend that Blacks were enticed by the notion of Oklahoma's Black towns as idealized places where Blacks could be free.[15] Nineteenth-century circulars and other recruiting devices beckoned Blacks in the South to settle towns in the West. Recruiters emphasized that the towns offered the kind of prosperity and relative freedom unavailable elsewhere in the country.[16] Town promoters tried to draw Southern-located Blacks away from their communities by stressing the unique and desirable possibilities that towns offered Black Americans in a racially threatening and divisive post-Emancipation period.[17] In their early years, Black-town newspapers announced the material goods (e.g., land and homes), economic stability, and quality-of-life factors (e.g., community, elevated social status, freedom) that a Black person could gain by making the move.[18]

Historians who tell the story of Black towns talk about how some Black-town promoters were Black intellectuals, activists, and political figures. For the movement to the West, Black activist Benjamin "Pap" Singleton is perhaps best known for the fifty thousand Blacks he motivated to settle in Kansas, Illinois, Missouri, and Indiana.[19] For Oklahoma, it was Edwin P. McCabe, who fulfilled this role when he served as treasurer of Logan County in what was then Oklahoma Territory. McCabe called for ten thousand Blacks to participate in the western land run, to form "all-Negro communities," and, ultimately, to turn the territory into an all-Black state. The notices that he circulated stressed the availability of "free land," the ability to build homes, and the opportunity to forge safe all-Black spaces. McCabe cast the West as a special place where Black dreams were possible.[20] Through his activism, Black towns were imagined as places where unique things could happen for Negro-identified Americans rarely afforded such opportunities elsewhere. McCabe's efforts spawned the early western Black town of **Langston**, where my grandparents and mother lived. More broadly, his work was one part of the trajectory that saw the establishment of more than fifty Black towns in what became the state of Oklahoma in 1907, out of more than two hundred such towns in the country.[21]

McCabe and other recruiters are not the only ones who extolled the unique virtues of Black towns. Historians and other scholars have posited Black towns as remarkable places.[22] They discuss how, over a period of approximately twenty-five to thirty years, Black towns became active, self-supporting communities that were models of Black economic and social vibrancy.[23] Scholars describe how town founders and residents created schools, banks, churches, insurance companies, and countless Black-owned business districts in these spaces.[24] Black-town businesses supported not only Black residents; they were also frequented by White consumers, even though the communities were populated almost exclusively by Blacks.[25] Because of this level and impact of entrepreneurship, scholars have described Black towns as flourishing models of Black American community-building, economic success, and social cohesion during the height of the towns' entrepreneurial activity and peak population.[26] Among scholars and others who tell the story of Black-town history, this period of success is almost always situated between the 1880s and the 1930s. In most accounts, the communities' demise was cinched by such events as the Great Depression, the decline in agriculture, and rising racial hostility that pervaded Oklahoma.[27] For some, the biggest evidence of Black towns' decline was the large-scale outmigration that saw Black towners heading to other parts of the United States and North America.[28]

This particular history of Black towns—as having had a successful three- to five-decade run—is vital to the overall Black-town story. For most people who know of Black towns, what happened in the past *is* the Black-town story. And yet, this book is not about the history of Black towns, their formation, their success, or their struggles in the first five decades of Black-town existence. Historians have documented multiple dimensions of that fascinating history,[29] shaping the perspective of Black towns as exceptional models of Black-community success that Black Americans actively sought out for a few decades. Another dimension of the Black-town story that is equally significant yet little explored is the continued draw of the towns in the twenty-first century. Focusing on the years 2004 to 2012 (the years leading up to and through the first term of the Obama presidency), this book takes up the question of what accounts for that appeal.

It is true that only thirteen of the fifty Oklahoma Black towns remain today, and among those that still exist, the population is scant (typically not exceeding one thousand residents per town and, in some cases, under one hundred). Generally, in the surviving towns, the Black-town economy is fragile and the local business base small to nonexistent. Based on median household income data from the 2010 census, several towns meet the official measure of poverty. And yet it is common to see a set of people living well and pursuing ambitious projects for economic development in a Black town. It is common to see a well-attended festival and busloads of tourists. It is also possible to find people who willfully—and excitedly—move into Black towns. Despite Black towns' classification as geographically, economically, and socially marginal places (due to their rural location, economic status, and the class and racial composition of the population), a significant number of people (not all of whom are Black) are drawn to the communities. Black towns remain alluring places where a variety of economic and social activities, interactions, and planning for the future occur. How are Black towns spaces of interest in the twenty-first century? Who is drawn to them? How and why?

Black-Town Senses of Place

Today, the idea of an impoverished and Black-identified place as a space of interest seems hard to grasp due to how we tend to think about blackness and place. The very term "Black community"—especially but not only when preceded with the word "poor"—most often conjures up a place to avoid, fear, or fix, not usually a place that you are excited to connect with. The blighted Black "inner city" marked by violence, crime, unemployment, and physical devastation is set firmly in the American mind. Over the past several decades, numerous studies and programs documenting these types of conditions or devising strategies to remedy them contribute to our sense of the perils and problems of a Black place.[30] Even Black middle-class communities do not escape this imagery. Due to racism and racial inequality, the conditions experienced in low-income Black communities exist in middle-class ones also and give us a sense that there is a ubiquity to Black devastated and unappealing places.[31] And although Black elite communities come closer to living out our notion of the American, suburban, middle-class dream and have the potential to complicate our notion of Black places, these communities remain outliers, distinct from the larger Black lower-income and middle-class reality. They are rarely represented to us. In fact, there has been little interest in researching Black elite communities. Sociologist Karyn Lacy has shown that members of a relatively high-income Black suburb in Washington, D.C., went to great lengths to successfully maintain their distance from middle-class and lower-middle-class Black neighborhoods, thereby safeguarding a different and upscale Black-community identity.[32] Yet, even with this relatively rare case and others like it that are little-known and little-studied, the resulting picture is that, in today's world, appealing places that bear the label "predominantly Black" or "Black communities" are few and far between.

This picture was challenged in 2015, when the notion of an ideal and alluring Black space was captured in a video sketch, *Negrotown*, performed by the comedy duo Key and Peele. Amid heightened national discussion of police brutality against African American males, the skit underscored how visions for attaining secure Black spaces live on in the twenty-first century. The sketch begins with Keegan-Michael Key, who plays an unnamed, casually dressed Black man, walking down a dark alley. He is stopped by the police and, during a verbal disagreement about the fairness of the stop, is physically assaulted by an officer. At the moment that Key's character dizzily stumbles from a knock on the head by the cop, another unnamed Black man, played by filmmaker and comedian Jordan Peele, emerges from a pile of debris in the alley, wearing a tattered flannel shirt and jeans. Based on his appearance and location, an easy assumption is that this seemingly disheveled man is homeless. But yet, with a broad smile on his face and a lilt in his voice, he surprisingly projects, "Alright officer, I'll take it from here!" The officer returns the smile as if the two have a well-rehearsed operation, removes the handcuffs from Key's character, and says happily, "All yours!" In disbelief and confusion, Key asks Peele, "Where are we going?," to which Peele replies, "I'm glad you asked!" Suddenly, as they push through a door in the alley, they are transported to a sunlit field. Peele's character, now wearing a bright peach-colored suit with a bow tie, skips along and begins singing in rhymes, reminiscent of a 1950s Broadway musical:

Follow me to a place I know
where there ain't no pain and no sorrow
It's the place to be if your skin is brooooowwwwnnnnn [pause]
I'm talking about Negrotown!

The peach-suited Peele, singing all the while, walks Key's still-confused character through a brilliant community with smiling Black people bustling about, brightly painted buildings, and nicely paved roads. There's no harassment in *Negrotown*, Peele's character explains in song. Resources are accessible. Taxis will pick you up. You can shop without being followed, and you can wear a hoodie freely. "I think I get it," Key's character says, excited. "It's like a utopia for Black people!" "Yeah!" Peele replies before belting out more details about the joys of life for brown-skinned people in *Negrotown*.

ALTHOUGH A FICTIONAL and comedic account, the sketch is an entrée into thinking about liberating Black spaces and the attraction they hold. As sociologists Marcus Hunter and Zandria Robinson point out, *Negrotown* "reflects a fantastical longing for a place where black people can be free."[33] In the late nineteenth and early twentieth centuries, Black towns were viewed like the fictional *Negrotown*,[34] places about which Black people marveled for the possibilities of free and Black-affirming living. In the twenty-first century, I argue, Black towns retain some of that marvel, an allure marked more by an interest in connecting with the significance of the towns' noteworthy past and the engaging possibilities for their future. Thus, Black towns today may not boast the extensive social and material riches of a *Negrotown*, but they are spaces for imagining grander possibilities and asserting Black worth.

I liken *Negrotown* to a concept by geographer Katherine McKittrick,[35] who discusses the motivators, qualities, and development of a "Black sense of place." The term draws from well-known geographer Doreen Massey's "global sense of place": how local places are infused with a range of global influences.[36] The term also resonates with the idea from *Senses of Place*, a book edited by anthropologists Steven Feld and Keith Basso that explores different examples of how people interact with and derive meaning from places.[37] For McKittrick, a *Black* sense of place is an idea of place that foregrounds Black freedom and refuses the inequality that Black people have encountered in countless lived spatial experiences.[38] McKittrick references the plantation as a significant and enduring site of spatial inequality, domination, and violence that a Black sense of place works against. The "auction block, the big house, the fields and crops, the slave quarters, the transportation ways leading to and from the plantation"—all are sites of space-delimited violence which, she tells us, exist within the plantation complex.[39] The violence of the plantation, on the one hand, is physical brutality, but on the other hand it is also the rendering of Black people at once placeless and contained, restricted and without the right to be rooted in a particular place.

A Black sense of place gestures toward an alternative to these conditions. As McKittrick puts it, "The violence of displacement and bondage, produced within a plantation economy, extends and *is given a geographic future*" (my emphasis).[40] In other words, in a Black approach to place, for McKittrick, experiences with spatial inequality (that have their roots in the plantation experience) are turned into a different spatial experience — a geographic future. The geographic future of plantation violence is spatial freedom, freedom in place.

What is an example of such a future? If you think about the Black town to which my uncle fled when he sought to escape everyday racial aggression in his Alabama town, Black towns were that future. Based on how my mother told the story, I suspect Uncle Buddy imagined that the towns would not constrain him, as a Black person. Black towns, as I believe he dreamed of them, embodied the Black sense of place that *extended a different geographic future* beyond the racial constraints of his Alabama town and the broader American South.

Particularly since the colonial period in the United States, we have examples where people of African descent have looked to places that can serve as sanctuaries.[41] Participants in these types of community-building projects have sought to opt out of circumstances that have marginalized and threatened them — a departure that represents a dream of Black self-determination made possible by the invention of a space that is communitarian and democratic.[42] In these spaces, Blacks especially in the Americas sought to build institutions that provide income, goods, relationships, and services for the embattled population and, by extension, safety and security. Indeed, beyond Black towns we can locate a Black sense of place in the founding of maroon villages (also known as communities of runaway slaves) that were established by enslaved African escapees who fled the bondage and aggression of colonialism and the plantation.[43] As Neil Roberts tells us, maroon life — itself a subversive space — *is* freedom from marginality.[44] A Black sense of place can also be found in the ways people of African descent in the Anglophone Caribbean took to communities known as Free Villages, which offered Afro-Caribbeans an exit option from restrictive labor contracts and the general repressive structure of post-Emancipation Caribbean plantations.[45] A Black sense of place can be found in the making of "Black Wall Streets" in Tulsa, Chicago, and Durham, North Carolina, where Black Americans created vibrant urban business districts during the legalized segregation that closed off opportunities for Blacks to achieve financial growth and wealth. It can be found in the making of Soul City, North Carolina, the 1970s community masterminded by Civil Rights activist Floyd McKissick, who sought federal funding to build a self-sustaining Black community. For McKissick, Soul City would remove African Americans from oppression in White-dominated society and the weight of urban decay.[46] A Black sense of place, then, is seen in these "alternative mappings,"[47] localities that demonstrate a perspective on place informed by and resistant to spatial inequality. In *Chocolate Cities*, Hunter and Robinson remind us, "Black people in the U.S. have moved, shifted, responded, resisted and created town and neighborhood spaces where they could be both Black and free."[48]

We could argue that other Black spaces are responses to different but related dynamics. Gentrification, redlining, redistricting, urban renewal, and the prison industrial complex—to name some—are all instances of spatial violence because they spatially marginalize, contain, and displace Black people. They are processes both resulting from and causing what sociologists and geographers call the "racialization of space," which is the hierarchical and unequal arrangement and treatment of spaces by race. In the United States, Black and Brown people are more apt to live in marginal spaces due to the ways that space is racially and unequally divided, by policy and practice.[49] This is also a form of spatial violence. Indeed, McKittrick thinks of the plantation as a prototype for other structures of spatial violence and argues that "blackness is an unspeakably intelligible trait within the [broad] practice of geographic violence in the Americas." In the way of such broad "practices of geographic violence" emerge Black enclaves, collectives, and movements. These are alternative, separate spaces, or spaces within the interstices of other spaces. They include Black cultural meccas, neighborhoods like Harlem in New York and Bronzeville in Chicago. Yet they also include spaces in an urban gentrifying or fragile neighborhood where community members come together to dream and organize for better futures and conditions, or to assert Black rights to recognition in the face of repressive projects.[50]

How does a Black sense of place play out? What does it look like? To address these questions requires considering that spaces are not fixed in place or static.[51] They are continuously made, hold diverse meanings to diverse people, and are experienced in a variety of contexts and by a range of people.[52] Therefore, a Black sense of place is not a singular sense of place. McKittrick tells us, "It is precisely within our collective plantation futures that fractured and multiple (Black and non-Black) perspectives on place and belonging are fostered and debated. A Black sense of place is not a steady, focused, and homogeneous way of seeing and being in place, but rather a set of changing and differential perspectives that are illustrative of, and therefore remark upon, legacies of normalized racial violence that calcify, but do not guarantee, the denigration of black geographies and their inhabitants."[53] A Black sense of place plays out in diverse, uneven, and dynamic ways. Even when places like Black towns uphold and organize the community for equality, inclusion, and affirmation, those principles may be challenged. A Black space that strives for inclusivity and affirmation of blackness must contend with spaces and forces that disrupt that project.[54] Indeed, there is a dialectic—a back and forth—between alternative Black spaces and the forces they resist. Put another way, the Black sense of place encompasses the spatial violence that it works against.[55] There are also differences in perspectives and visions due to the diverse positions of people, who are Black and non-Black, in that space.

Thus, a Black place is not a utopia. The tensions around spatial inequality throw into question possibilities for an idyllic Black place. Making this point, the *Negrotown* sketch ends with Key's character—after having believed he was in a "utopia for Black people"—waking up to find out that the place was an illusion and that he is being arrested by the officer who gave him the knock on the head. The lesson is that a Black utopia like *Negrotown* is only possible in our imagination.[56] A similar point rings through in Toni Morrison's *Paradise*, a fictional account of Oklahoma Black towns, as Morrison shows us that the "Havens" Black people set out to create cannot completely evade falling victim to or even re-creating the inequalities that led to the communities' conceptualization and formation in the first place.[57]

However, it is at the intersection of this desire for a free Black space and the forces that work to challenge that desire where Black people who are committed to alternative and free-existence communities sometimes dig in their heels. They demand their rights to recognition and nonessentialist representations.[58] They critique and refuse injurious programs purported to fix their communities.[59] They assert their narratives of heritage and Black mobility against other narratives that might mute that experience.[60] They proclaim the influence of their underrecognized place across the country.[61] In Black towns, as folks struggle with rural gentrification, a neoliberal economy, and the material marginality of rural America, residents and town leaders work to create new and better economies that resonate with the success of the Black-town economic past. In contrast to narratives of Oklahoma's history that efface Blacks' contribution, tour guides of Black-town history tell a narrative of Black success and significance in the state. In contrast to depictions of Black communities as fractured and rural Black communities as removed from contemporary life, Black-town festivals perform blackness and Black-town life as modern places.

Black towns are imagined places. New residents, tourists, and event participants come to Black towns for their idea of a Black experience, hoping to learn about Black greatness in the past, to connect with that greatness, or to commune with people who are drawn to or living where Black greatness is centered, publicly displayed, and valued. And even more, people and institutions come to Black towns with a vision to remake them—either by taking them out of their impoverishment and restoring them through a development plan, or by profiting from their poverty through investment schemes. Even today, when Black towns are not a Western mecca in the way they were one hundred years ago, the communities continue to reflect Black people's ideas about what they would like the space to be and represent. You can see these ideas in the narratives they tell to tourists, the festivals they present to the public, the histories they tell of their communities and families, and the economic-improvement projects they invest in. In the same way that, according to sociologist George Lipsitz, a "Black spatial imaginary" is a Black concept of place that elevates democracy and inclusion as well as Black rights and belonging, a Black-town imagination argues for these things as well.[62] Lipsitz discusses Black people in New Orleans street parades moving and interacting freely in public spaces, countering Black containment or exclusion and demonstrating a right to the city. In the chapters that follow, you will see a Black-town imaginary that situates Black towns and Black people ubiquitously—rather than contained in the past or in poor, rural spaces—and calling for inclusivity, Black prominence and affirmation, rights and belonging.

The appeal of Black towns for Black people is found in the towns' capacity, as places deemed historically significant, to enable ideas about what those communities can be. The towns also enable actions to serve those ideas. Put more simply, the Black-town past—as a notable Black past—has allowed people to imagine and work on the towns as spaces of possibility, mobility, alternative futures, and sociality. Such an engagement with Black towns is, in part, a political move to the extent that it lays claims and offers an appeal about what Black life can and should be. For Blacks associating with Black towns, the narrative of a place that saved Blacks from racial terror and enabled a rise in Blacks' social status allows them, implicitly and explicitly, to elevate and retell that history as one of Black success and citizenship and to think about and argue for Black future success. We will see people narrating Black-town life, imagining Black-town possibilities, and acting them out by leveraging Black-town history and racial identity to intervene in common discourses about Black communities and Black life in general. In doing so, they often seek to create something better.

However, they may also expose and critique inequality that Blacks experience to underscore Blacks' rights. Indeed, you will see that people disagree about what life in Black towns should be like. A variety of people (of different generations, races, and social status) and institutions (both local and "external" to Black towns) are drawn to the communities, and they bring different ways of imagining this space. They bring different ways of interacting with the space. As McKittrick said, a geographic future that is the crux of a Black sense of place encompasses "Black and non-Black perspectives on place and belonging," which are in tension with one another.[63] For example, some Black people want to build up Black-town economies to restore the communities' vibrancy and the regard people have for them, while others (especially non-Blacks) want to profit from their current economic vulnerability. At the center of ensuing debates about how to chart Black-town futures and invest in Black towns are questions about the place of Black towns—and Black people more generally—in history, America, economies, and society.

A Brief Profile of Oklahoma's Black Towns

I set out to do research on Oklahoma's Black towns with the caution and concern of my East Coast friends who feared that, as a Black person, I might be stepping into a state with few Black people. I heard "be careful" a few times. When many who are unfamiliar with the state think of Oklahoma's population, they think of American Indian heritage and politically and socially conservative Whites. But the truth is that Oklahoma has a rich and significant Black presence, with a little over 7 percent of the population identifying as Black or African American in the 2000 and 2010 U.S. censuses.[64] This is below the national average, but half of the states in the country have fewer Blacks than Oklahoma. With the exception of Oklahoma's panhandle, where the Black presence is especially sparse, Black communities can be found in urban and rural areas all across the state. In the state's two largest cities, Oklahoma City and Tulsa, the Black population is highest, and in some midsize cities or suburbs, Blacks represent as much as 23 percent of residents.[65] For particular small cities, like Muskogee and Guthrie, where Blacks have had a presence since at least the early twentieth century and have maintained active business areas, the Black population currently is slightly higher than the national average.[66] In Muskogee, Blacks make up 16 percent of the population, and in Guthrie they are 14 percent.[67]

People in Black towns who identified as Black or African American between 2000 and 2010 made up a majority of the population in most cases. With the exception of two Black towns, the 2000 population in Black towns was over 55 percent Black, and half the towns had a Black population of

75 percent or higher. This was true in 2010 as well. However, for those towns with a Black population falling below 75 percent, three towns had a Black population that was less than half.[68] The slight whitening of Black towns, which will be discussed in chapter 3 and the epilogue, most likely contributes to this shift over a decade. However, it is also important to acknowledge that the population averages, by race, are skewed due to the very small size of the towns. The numbers are also impacted by institutions within some towns. For example, in **Boley** and **Taft**, which house correctional facilities, the prison population is counted in census data. In **Langston**, location of a historically Black university, the student population that may be resident in the town is also counted. Thus, census data can give the impression that non-Blacks—especially Whites, who are the highest-represented population after Blacks in Black towns—have a bigger presence in Black towns than they actually have in everyday life. In fact, Black-town residents and leaders sometimes question the veracity of census data to account for who lives in their community.

These kinds of questions about who lives in Black towns and what that lived experience is all about was my concern when I set out to research Black towns. For eight years, between 2004 and 2012, I researched race, place, and meaning in the Oklahoma communities. As a cultural anthropologist, I spent much time observing town life, attending town and organization meetings, going to church, touring town facilities and institutions, participating in annual events, joining tourist activities, and engaging with residents (former and current). With the help of two research assistants, I collected more than one hundred interviews of people who live in Black towns, used to live in Black towns, visit Black towns (as tourists especially), or have some connection to Black towns through work or social associations. I focused my observations and interviews especially on four Black towns that I call Freeland, Newtown, Promise, and Wrightsville. (I use pseudonyms for the towns to protect the identities of the people who you will meet in the following pages.) The towns have much in common, but there are some important distinctions among them. Among Black towns, Freeland and Promise are medium- and small-sized communities, respectively. Because Black towns are quite small, with populations sometimes under seventy-five and rarely over one thousand, Freeland is in the middle of the range and Promise is on the lower end. The two towns sit in eastern Oklahoma among the cluster of towns near the seat of the Creek Nation; Creek lands were the basis for their origins, as is true of a majority of remaining Black towns located in that area. Newtown and Wrightsville are larger towns, located west of that region.

Although my research focused on four particular towns, I looked at all thirteen of the remaining Black towns. In addition to visiting almost all of them, I attended meetings where representatives from several of the towns were present. Black-town mayors belong to networks such as the Oklahoma Council of Black Mayors (OCBM). At the OCBM meetings I attended, Black-town mayors shared vital information about their town projects and initiatives. They talked about grants they were writing, town clean-up efforts they were spearheading, and efforts to promote their communities. Indeed, it was at the OCBM meetings that I not only gained insights into the activities and concerns of individual towns; I also learned about the existence and significance of a community of Black towns. Additionally, I studied the unincorporated satellite communities that surround Promise, Newtown, Wrightsville, and Freeland. These are towns like Kidder, a satellite of Newtown; and King's Prairie and Jewel, satellites of Freeland. In most instances, Black-town satellite communities use their "host town" (Promise, Newtown, Wrightsville, or Freeland) as the town identified in their formal postal address. Yet they are informally and practically speaking recognized by other unofficial names. They also have distinct geographic boundaries that are understood by those who live in the area. They are separate communities, then, at the same time that they interface with the town to which they are formally attached. In fact, the count of existing Black towns should be higher than thirteen when we consider these unincorporated settlements that surround incorporated Black towns. You will encounter these settlements in this book, and you will also encounter communities like Green Valley (a Black-town tour location) and Pineway (a predominantly White town neighboring Promise), as well as **Boley**, **Taft**, **Langston**, and **Rentiesville**. (When I refer to Black towns by their actual names to discuss public and known events that occurred in them, I place them in bold type. I don't use bold type for the pseudonyms.) Talking about this range of communities in a book focused on Black towns, I am arguing that, to talk of Black towns—especially what makes them appealing and to whom—requires thinking broadly and beyond the geographic boundaries that we often affix to place.

To that point, you will also encounter Tulsa and Oklahoma City as well as smaller Oklahoma cities like Guthrie and Muskogee. And you will hear about Kansas City, Houston, and Los Angeles. Rural towns like Black towns may be considered remote, but people in Black towns travel. They migrate to other Southern and Midwestern cities, where they may live for the bulk of their adult lives, all the while going back and forth to visit family and attend social events. Town events bring people from far and wide. Rural employment is limited, and so people in Black towns commute. They work in Oklahoma City, Tulsa, or Muskogee, or in one of the university towns such as Norman or Stillwater. Even tourists of Black towns learn about the towns on tours that go outside the town borders. Although it is common to talk about the vast and fast movement in the global economy, movement and networks also mark rural domestic places like Black towns, as the travel and economic activities surrounding them show.[69] In fact, due to the kinds of industries, economic structures, migrations, and even cultural influences that are part of Black-town life, Black towns are global, which will also become apparent in the pages ahead.

After graduating from high school, many Black-town residents leave the communities to pursue employment elsewhere because the sentiment is that work in the towns has dried up. Many people are likely to return after they retire, drawn back to the place they call home, or returning to care for an elderly parent, as anthropologist Carol Stack described for Blacks in rural North Carolina who migrated to the Northeast and then returned to their homes in the South.[70] In this sense, Black towns are the picture of rural America, marked by heavy outmigration, return migration, economic fragility, an aging population, ailing or nonexistent agriculture and industry, and a decline in local businesses alongside a heavy reliance on major retail establishments like Costco and Target.[71] What many call the neoliberal economy—with its emphasis on free markets and privatization as well as its disinvestment from social services and reliance on cheap labor[72]—is central to the contemporary Black-town experience. The neoliberal economy has much to do with the current economic fragility of Black towns. However, as economically fragile rural places, Black towns are appealing to investors and to the state for profit-making ventures. They are certainly appealing to big-box stores like Walmart, which is the recipient of so many Black-town consumer dollars.

Again, this picture of economic devastation is a common rural American story, as is a story about rural America being White. Indeed, 78 percent of the rural U.S. population is White, while 9 percent is Hispanic, 8 percent is Black, and under 2 percent Asian and Native American.[73] Yet racially, rural Black towns in Oklahoma are predominantly Black. It is not just checking a box on the census; the vast majority of people in the towns told us they identify as Black or African American, even though many said they have some Native American ancestry that they have not officially claimed on the U.S. Census, in tribal enrollment applications, or elsewhere. As one woman from

Wrightsville told me as a way of explaining why she does not claim her Native American ancestry, "It ain't never done nothing for me." This woman saw no value in such a claim even though her family had a narrative about their Indian roots. Others told me that they abandoned attempts to prove, with records, their family's tribal membership even though they had some degree of evidence. Hearing these accounts made me think about the also widely held belief among African Americans that, in moving through life in America, a Black identity supersedes all others, even in a so-called mixed-race person. In fact, at the time of my research, Freedmen's membership in Oklahoma's Cherokee Nation was being challenged due to their blackness or inability to prove biological (rather than social) ancestry.[74] However, some Black towners' seeming reluctance to claim American Indian identity also provides an explanation for why the Native American bases of Black towns are now practically invisible, and why some might say that Black towns are "just Black."

About 2 percent to 10 percent of Black-town residents identify as American Indian on the U.S. Census, which amounts to an average of two households per town.[75] And although the U.S. Census shows that Whites in some towns represent as much as 50 percent of the population, those numbers are skewed.[76] Indeed, in each Black town that I studied, there are a few Whites who are permanent residents and several Whites who are visiting partners (frequent visitors) of Black residents. The numbers appear to be growing, but for the period of my study, Whites were still a minority and not considered representative of the town demographics. In fact, people in Black towns will tell you that their community is predominantly Black, and based on my research I agree.

The communities' racial composition is only part of the reason why blackness is significant to Black towns. Black towns are like many Black communities, urban or rural; they experience challenges like structural inequality that leaves their communities with disproportionate rates of underemployment, inadequate housing, and crime. Also, like so many Black communities, they take pride in the successes of their professional class or in their community members' achievements, wanting to revere their significant histories, or dreaming and planning for better futures. Countless studies have shown us these features in many Black communities.[77] Black towns are no different. They are Black communities, linked experientially to other Black communities in America.

But, beyond being connected to other Black communities, the towns that we will journey to in the next pages are also like communities everywhere:

diverse, mobile, and unbounded. The Black-town population can be put into categories such as Black or African American; however, the population includes a range of identities. People in Black towns come from different generations, hold different occupations, have differing partnership statuses, and have different opinions about their towns and also about their state and the country. In some way, though, most of them—regardless of social identity—express some idea about the appealing qualities of their community. You might hear it in the way they talk about what the town is. Or you might understand it when they talk about what the town was or what they want it to be. It is also possible that you'll appreciate this sentiment when they engage with, think about, and connect with the town. That the towns are appealing might also strike you in the reactions and comments of those who visit, work in, or know about the towns. However, as you take in these perspectives over the next few chapters, remember that the appeal of Black towns is not simplistic. It cannot be summed up in a catchy slogan boasting the virtues of the community. Remember that being an alluring Black place has its challenges, and this is the reality and conundrum of a twenty-first-century Black town.

CHAPTER ONE

History Stories

It is hard to visit an Oklahoma Black town without encountering a narrative about the town's history. In each town's center, there is signage with information about the development of Black towns in the state and the origins of that particular town. In the 1990s, the Oklahoma History Center, an affiliate of the Smithsonian and Oklahoma's primary authority on state history, created those bold red and green signs, which continue to occupy a prominent place in each of the thirteen towns. "Nowhere else . . . did African American men and women come together to live in and govern their own communities," the signs announce. "The All-Black towns were established on the rich topsoil of the new territory and state . . . [they] prospered until the 1920s but gradually declined under the pressure of Jim Crow laws . . . the Great Depression, and population flight from farm to city after World War I."

The sign's last sentence is the only part that mentions current conditions: "Today a few All-Black towns survive but all are remembered, a legacy of economic and political freedom." And yet, while the statement about Black towns' history from the eighteenth century to the early twentieth century elevates the past as a way to define what Black towns *were*, the signs also define what Black towns *are*. The idea that all towns are embedded in the state's memory ("Black towns survive but all are remembered") is a signal that the Black-town past survives in the present. Additionally, the sign's content and language draw on the currency of contemporary discourses about race, particularly narratives of Black success.

For many consumers as well as state producers of Black heritage narratives in the twenty-first century, much of the attraction of a story about Black history is the story's emphasis on Black people's prominence, triumph, or resilience in the past,[1] even if those stories also include struggle. Narratives of Black triumph and progress can mitigate the trauma of taking in a gritty account of struggle. Or they can provide empowerment to the narrative's consumers, especially consumers from socially marginal groups.[2] As anthropologist Bayo Holsey reminds us, triumph narratives about a particular aspect of Black history "[transform] what might otherwise be a story of unadulterated misery that many would rather forget into a story that can be collectively

Oklahoma History Center's Black-town sign in **Tatums**,
Oklahoma. Photo by author.

remembered and celebrated."[3] Indeed, the History Center signs inform us
that Black towns are marked by a number of noteworthy historic achievements. People who formed Black towns developed communities character-
ized by economic vibrancy and self-sufficiency ("they prospered until the
1920s"), freedom ("[they] governed their own communities," and the towns
are a "legacy of economic and political freedom"), a pioneering spirit ("established on . . . the new territory and state"), community ("they [came]

together"), and security (because Black towns "declined under the pressure of Jim Crow laws"—a signal that, as a thriving community of Black people, they were safe from racial hostility until segregation laws were put in place). Perhaps these features hold sway because, on the one hand, stories of Black American success fulfill a post–Civil Rights yearning for examples in which obstacles to racial progress are not foregrounded. On the other hand, success narratives give Black people agency and affirm their worth, setting straight counterclaims about disorganized or deficient Black culture. Black scholars and activists have been significant contributors to the work of vindicationism, refuting narratives of Black deficiency with evidence of Black achievement.[4]

Among academics, historians have given us the most in this area, helping to identify history as the most significant facet of Black-town existence.[5] Others also have contributed to an affirmation of Black-town history as a story of success. They include people working for museums and libraries, historic preservation groups, and archivists who often document or exhibit Black-town history as a remarkable history. They also include town residents, particularly elders, who serve as local historians of Black-town life.

It is true that historical narratives about Black towns often acknowledge challenges and do not paint a picture of a struggle-free Black community. Indeed, the Black-town-history story is a story of community-making in the midst of and against racial inequality and violence. Yet, ultimately, Black-town-history stories—as told by the Oklahoma History Center, but also by many scholars—are not stories that center on enslavement, lynching, or Black people pursued by the Klan. They are not stories of sharecroppers stuck in debt peonage, of menial wage-laborers barely able to eke out an existence, or undereducated Black people attending underfunded schools. They are not stories of people living in shacks, tenements, or ghettos. Instead, they are the stories of Blacks who mostly thrived. That is the Black-town-history story that you will hear from many sources, in many ways, and supplemented with many different anecdotes. The narrative counters the more pervasive Black-struggle narrative that has higher currency in the United States. The Black-town-history story is why people—as we will see—tour Black towns, work on revitalizing Black towns, and move to Black towns: to be consumers of and participants in Black greatness, which vindicates Black people and obstructs narratives of Black pathology.

Unspeakable Terror, Running for Their Lives

My mother's story about Uncle Buddy's ascent is a Black-town-history story that extends beyond him. The first part of the story, about his displacement and anger wrought by the racial hostility of the Deep South at the hands of a White man, is what eventually connects Uncle Buddy to a Black town. My research assistants and I heard this story arc multiple times, from people who lived in Black towns and also, like me, from people who heard it from their own parents about either their parents' experience, their grandparents' experience, or the experience of some other kin. I can't say that we heard such stories from a majority of elders who talked of their family origins in a Black towns. But we heard it enough times for it to feel like a pattern. In the stories, Black towns are where people fled to, in search of a safer, better existence. Yet, for this part of the accounts, the emphasis is less on what Black towns afforded fleeing kin and more on the terror of the South that prompted urgent flight to the West. In fact, the South figures prominently as the starting point for a family's move to a Black town in the West. The Deep South was the antithesis of the Western Black town because, in the stories we heard, it was where eventual Black towners encountered hostility due to their Black identities. Yet, unlike in the account that I was told about my great uncle, many of the racially charged Deep South encounters that people told my research assistants and me involved *unspeakable* terror. In my uncle's case, the hostility involved a White barber taking away his livelihood. In several other cases that we heard, the hostility was so extreme that it threatened the life of an elder or deceased kin of the narrator. It was hostility so intense that it was difficult for the story narrator—talking about the near-death of their kin—to get out, or difficult for their parents to tell them about. In these stories, people are quite literally running for their lives and the lives of their family members. They faced the threat of being lynched. They witnessed or were involved in a murder. They were told or had credible evidence that they would be killed. The greatness of the Black town was its refuge from this terror.

In an interview, I first heard such an account from Mrs. Jessup, an elder in Wrightsville whom almost everyone I encountered insisted that I talk to. Due to her age and also her prominence in the community, she was considered a deep repository of knowledge about Wrightsville's history. At the time of our interview, she was in her seventies, and she didn't hesitate to accept my request to meet. She ushered me into her home and had me sit down in an armchair across from the large, tweed, La-Z-Boy-style recliner where she sat, looking relaxed. I would sit in that chair for two consecutive days, listening to her tell me about Wrightsville, late into the evening on a Tuesday and again on a Wednesday, when she finished up. That Tuesday was another scorching-hot day in Oklahoma. Mrs. Jessup had two standing fans turned up high and, as we spoke, she sometimes asked me to reposition one or both of them so that the air was circulating better and keeping her cool. "I don't know why I feel so warm," she commented, as she went on telling me stories, undeterred by the heat.

In telling her story of how her family came to Wrightsville and what she experienced as a resident, Mrs. Jessup wove in others' stories, acknowledging that how people got their start in Wrightsville was not a uniform process. For her parents, educational opportunities took them to Wrightsville. But she recalled the story of the man considered the founder of her parents' school, who was also her distant relative and ran a funeral home in town. He came to Wrightsville to escape threats to his life, she said. "See, what happened, uh, they [the man and his family] come from the south of Texas or somewhere, and one of them, when they got to Wrightsville, officially they changed their name 'cause I think there'd been a killing or something down there where they come, and running, you know. People would get away sometime."

The man's story was part of Wrightsville lore that Mrs. Jessup, like others from her generation, had heard over the years. In part, this aspect of his story was known widely because, as a major business owner, *he* was known widely. And so, I suspect, this is the reason that his story circulated. Indeed, not everyone's story of how they came to a Black town is widely known but, within families, stories were passed around. Mrs. Jessup told the man's story with relative ease—in what came across to me as a matter-of-fact telling. She didn't know all the facts since she told me that she *thought* "there'd been a killing *or something*. . . ." She saw escaping terror as a common narrative ("*People* would get away sometimes") and so, in some respects, she spoke both about the man's individual experience and also the experience of flight from Southern racial terror more generally. However, those who directly experienced unspeakable terror or, more likely, knew of it through their own immediate family, were apt to include more clarity and detail.

That was the case of Mr. Tinsdale of Newtown, who said that he often heard his grandfather tell stories of how he had to get out of Alabama (and ended up in Newtown) based on what he witnessed. "He left Alabama because he was—. He went down to the [cotton] gin to take a bale of cotton and a Black boy got into it down there with a White guy and they got to fighting and the Black guy took a single tree . . . off a wagon. [It's] [w]hat they hook the mules to, and he h—, hit that White guy across the head. . . . And [t]hey lynched [the Black guy's] whole family. And my granddad say, 'I'm getting out of here.'"

Others had stories about threats made directly to their family, not merely what their family saw happening to others. Mrs. Logan, who describes herself as three generations removed from slavery (her grandmother was born enslaved), told us about what happened to her great uncle in Texas, which influenced her parents to move to Oklahoma and eventually settle in Kidder, a small Black settlement on the outskirts of Newtown:

> My great uncle had hit a man, a White man down there, and so my
> grandmother, uh, he had been up in the, up in—. They had what they
> called a, what they—. It was a log—. You know, there was logging
> down there and what they did was cut wood and he was back up in
> those woods which was plenty of pine trees and stuff. And so, he was
> back up in there and they kept trying to get him out and he wouldn't
> turn himself in, you know. And so, my grandmother went and talked
> him into turning himself in, and what he did was he came down and
> they hung him. And after they hung him then they were going to hang
> my grandfather and, and mess with the family so there was a gentleman
> out in Kidder. . . . He came there and brought my grandfather and
> them—he knew my grandfather and them—he came and went and
> picked them up and brought them back here in a covered wagon, back
> in the day, and brought them to Kidder.

And in Promise, Mr. Simms, age seventy-four, explained how his parents came to live in Promise through the experience of his grandfather who had a run in "down South" with a sharecropper who mistreated him. Mr. Simms struggled to get the story out, acknowledging that his parents similarly struggled to share the account and their childhood in the Deep South with Mr. Simms and his siblings:

> If I can recall, my mother and father talking about their childhood,
> which they didn't talk too much, especially my father. He didn't talk
> too much about his childhood and, uh, he explained why. Uh, his
> daddy, they came outta somewhere in Louisiana. And, uh, uh, my, my
> great uncle, my daddy's uncle, was a sharecropper. [A]nd, uh, the, uh,
> this has been years and years ago, now. This is, this is the way it, it was
> told to us children. His uncle, uh, at the end of the harvest the, uh, the

White man that he was workin' for, sharecroppin' for, [gave them] so much percentage—of whatever it was he was raisin', cotton or corn or whatever, and he would always, uh, oh, misuse, I mean [mis]treat, my great uncle, and my great uncle had children. My dad was . . . about six years, six or seven years old. . . . So, the end of the story went that my great uncle, uh, got so upset and he got tired of being mistreated, misused, and he shot this White, uh, sharecropping guy. . . . That was way back. . . . And, uh—then . . . [the family] got into problems and trouble— . . . as a result of what my uncle did and, uh, . . . according to my dad, he left. He didn't even go back to the house— . . . They had bloodhounds and—well you've probably seen some of— . . . He, he knew that they, they was having problems with, uh, with the, uh, the White people because of what had happened. . . . But somehow, uh, . . . my father, along with his younger brother, somehow got on a freight train—if I'm remembering it correctly—and they came into, uh, Oklahoma.

Family members rising up against terror and then needing to escape to save their lives are the opener for the Black-town-history story that some elders in Black towns tell. The experiences that people recounted to us resonated across families and, in some cases, broke up families. These experiences of terror and mistreatment were the catalyst for Black Southerners searching for life elsewhere. However, just as narratives of history differ, you aren't likely to find Black-town-history stories of unspeakable terror in museum exhibits about Black towns, and, if you do, there won't be much elaboration.[6] You are more likely to find these accounts in other museums on Black history, like the Smithsonian's National Museum of African American History and Culture, or, of course, the National Memorial for Peace and Justice, also known as the National Lynching Museum. Even Tulsa's exhibits on the "Race riots" of 1921 recount the terror that Blacks experienced in the Greenwood community, along with the success of that community prior to the violence that devastated the neighborhood. However, the Black-town story is usually about what happened to and by people inside Black towns once they were living in the town borders. The textured details of what people experienced in the Deep South—the details that come when Black-town residents tell their families' Black-town origin stories—usually do not make it into public accounts. And yet, stories of unspeakable terror are indeed Black-history stories even though, in most "official" or public renderings of Black-town history, racial terror in the South is decoupled from the narratives of Black success.

Property and Businesses as the Stuff of Black Mobility and Respectability

The most ubiquitous Black-town-history story is one of Black *economic* success, achieved through the acquisition of property such as land and homes, and the running of Black-owned businesses. For the Oklahoma towns, that story became broadly and publicly consumed when the Black educator and activist Booker T. Washington penned a 1908 article about his visit to **Boley**. In fact, scholars and townspeople alike consider Washington the motivator of Black-town formation across the country.[7] His ideas about Black economic self-reliance, for which he advocated vociferously, are considered to have gained traction nationally and driven some Blacks to head to towns like **Boley** to fulfill his plan.[8] As the most robust and active Oklahoma Black town, **Boley** became emblematic of the type of economic activity that Washington encouraged and, writing about **Boley's** vibrancy, Washington helped brand the town as a success. In the article that appeared in *Outlook* magazine, he described individuals coming from the South and successfully starting businesses:

> It is a striking evidence of the progress made in thirty years that the present northward and westward movement of the negro people has brought into these new lands, not a helpless and ignorant horde of black people — but land-seekers and home-builders, men who have come prepared to build up the country. . . . One sees them everywhere, working side by side with white men. They have their banks, business enterprises, schools, and churches. . . . Immigrants, like Mr. T. R. Ringe, the mayor, who was born a slave in Kentucky, and Mr. E. L. Lugrande, one of the principal stockholders in the new bank, came out in the new country, like so many of the white settlers, merely to get land. Mr. Lugrande came from Denton County, Texas, where he had 58 acres of land. He had purchased this land some years ago for four and five dollars the acre. He sold it for fifty dollars an acre, and, coming to Boley, he purchased a tract of land just outside of town and began selling town lots. Now a large part of his acreage is in the center of the town. A large proportion of the settlers of Boley are farmers from Texas, Arkansas, and Mississippi. But the desire for western lands has drawn into the community not only farmers, but doctors, lawyers, and craftsmen of all kinds. The fame of the town has also brought, no doubt, a certain proportion of the drifting population. But

behind all other attractions of the new colony is the belief that here negroes would find greater opportunities and more freedom of action than they have been able to find in the older communities North and South.[9]

Among the most cited figures on Black towns, Washington's words appear on museum exhibit tableaus and in many of the online and popular writings about the communities. He is also profiled in Norman L. Crockett's oft-referenced 1979 classic book, which is aptly titled *The Black Towns*. Crockett devotes much of an entire chapter on Black-town "Economy and Society" to Washington, crediting him with sparking Black-towns' economic goals as well as commending Black towns from Mississippi to Oklahoma.[10] The chapter shows how Black-town promoters and leaders widely embraced and closely followed Washington. For Crockett, Washington was instrumental in motivating and shaping Black-town economies that were based on Blacks achieving self-sufficiency by developing an extensive business base in the towns.

The important part of this is that Washington's words and influence have been defining Black towns for a century, from the time that he was speaking and organizing nationally until the present, when explanations of Black-town formation in Oklahoma mention his institutional advocacy of Black economic self-reliance or his public reverence of **Boley**. Even though Crockett argued that Oklahoma's Black towns went against Washington's belief that Black investment should be in the South,[11] it is nonetheless true that Washington is frequently referenced to help explain *why* Oklahoma Black towns were remarkable and to suggest that Black towns everywhere were major economic engines.

WHAT IS MORE, Washington has remained influential in identifying Black economic success as an ingredient of Black social respectability. That is, that there were thriving Black businesses in the Jim Crow era is a testament to the rise in status of Black people who ran those businesses and lived in the towns where those businesses excelled. Washington talked about Black-town economies demonstrating "civilization" and "progress"; he spoke of Blacks "building up the country"—not "helpless" or "ignorant" Black people. Washington not only helped cement the idea that Black towns are about successful entrepreneurship; he also shaped a belief in Black towns as a vehicle for Black Americans to make a social ascent.

Another image that fed this notion of Black respectability is a photo of **Boley**. If you do a search for "Black town" or "**Boley**" on the internet, you are

Boley Town Council, circa 1907–1910.

likely to find this iconic image of eleven men standing in front of a building. Etched above them (apparently by the photographer) are the words "Members of Town Council, Boley, OK." Captions for the photo put the date at "circa 1907–1910." Even today, the photo is the one most often attached to newspaper, magazine, and online articles about Oklahoma Black towns. It appeared in an Al Jazeera News story on "Renewed Interest" in Oklahoma's Black Towns; on an Oklahoma public radio feature on "Why Oklahoma Black Towns Prospered while Most of Oklahoma's Indian Territory Faded Away"; on Blackamericaweb.com, associated with the popular Black radio program Tom Joyner Radio for its regular "Little Known Black History Fact" segment; as the lone image for the *Encyclopedia of the Great Plains* entry on "All-Black Towns";[12] and, of course, on Oklahoma Historical Society's webpage on **Boley**.[13]

The men stand posed for the photo. Suited up, most of them don ties with white button-down shirts and vests. Because they are in such formal attire, the photo conveys their elevated social status. At the same time, for some of the men, their posture is relaxed. Some are looking away, others with hands relaxed by their side or, with jackets open, hands in their pockets. Thus, the photo suggests both comfort and formality. Although the men are posed, their stance is not as formal as in a portrait, for example. Are they both respectable men of status *and* comfortable in their surroundings, a Black town?

These are the men of whom Booker T. Washington spoke when he mentioned "progress" and "civilization." That the people in the photo are all men also gives us the town's prominence as rooted in or dependent upon masculinity as leadership. Indeed, even allowing for conventions of gendered terminology at the time, it is hard to separate **Boley's** town motto since its founding, "All Men Up—Not Some Men Down," from this image of "all men" who appear to be (socially) "up." What is especially noteworthy is that this image—of a formal male leadership—is *the* image for Oklahoma Black towns. It continues to circulate much more often than images of the towns' small school buildings, or of the early twentieth-century Black-town homes that by twenty-first-century standards might not please our sensibilities of what an elite dwelling should look like. You can find photos of schools and homes as well as of other aspects of early Black-town life. Yet you will have to search harder to find photos of early twentieth-century Black-town buildings attached to an article or magazine story about Black-town history. In fact, images of modest buildings are more apt to appear in parts of a Black-town story that discuss and lament how the prestigious Black-town past no longer exists. In Black-town stories, broken-down buildings can serve as emblems of the Black-town present but not of Black-town history. Indeed, even on the Oklahoma Historical Society page, the encyclopedia entry for "Black Towns" has a photo of a modern-day map but no image of a town. Their entries for other Black towns usually have an image conveying high social standing: the one for the town of **Taft**, for example, shows formally dressed faculty in front of a school building. The images used in contemporary Black-town-history stories, then, define the places as Black, middle-class, and respectable, with some images speaking to these qualities having more currency and circulation than others.

In the stories townspeople tell, that history of status enhancement also matters. Acquiring land and building homes as a route to increased social status was part of Mrs. Jessup's Black-town family origin story. She stressed that land improved her family's status, but she spoke more generally about this dynamic as a community pattern:

People came, used to come, to Wrightsville from the farm to have a home in Wrightsville so their kids could go to school. And during . . . World War II, a lot of people moved here and built homes. I don't want to say a lot, well, a number of them — I'll say it like that — built . . . moved here and built homes. They bought land, and I remember a man used to sell a lot of land here. . . . He would go — . He worked around the courthouse in [the neighboring city] and he would — . Well you know when they have the, uh, tax sale for lots? He bought up a lot of lots and then he'd sell the people lots [to 'em] like for three dollars a lot, and my, that's how my mama got her lot, three dollars a lot. And you could pay him fifty cents down and fifty cents a month. . . . That's the way . . . they got, they bought lots and . . . some of them moved houses in on the lots. Most people moved . . . in, lots, I mean moved houses in, and, uh, if it was a man or husband or something that had a carpenter [mind] they would build their [homes].

The high social value placed on property (land and homes) resonates across all the towns. Black people could become property owners and renters in Black towns, and that was reason enough for the towns to become associated with Black freedom.[14] That point rings clear in the numerous stories people told us of how their family members came to a Black town because of a perception of land "availability," the chance to build a home on that land, and engage in work — especially farming or business ownership — without the obstacles my Uncle Buddy faced as an entrepreneur in Alabama.

In addition to talking about land and homes, people we interviewed often mentioned businesses, echoing Booker T. Washington's listing of Black-town establishments frequented by residents and visitors.[15] This is part of talk about the glory days. "We *had* doctors, and lawyers," a Black-town resident beamed as she gave me a short tour of the town. Others told me about the strips of businesses that lined their streets. Whereas the Oklahoma History Center and academic writings treat Black-town history as successful until about 1930, Black-town residents in the twenty-first century take that success later. In fact, when he documented Black-town businesses across small and large towns, Mozell Hill counted an average of thirty establishments per town in 1940.[16] He considered these numbers to be small and partial evidence of Black-town poverty at the time, but this perception is most likely due to an implicit comparison with urban areas and prior town activity. Indeed, Black-town residents we spoke to fondly reminisced about active stores, juke joints and clubs, and services into the 1970s. Describing

Wrightsville's heyday as having ended about three decades ago, Mrs. Jessup rattled off a bunch of businesses that were in the town. She came to this list after I asked her to tell me what she meant when she said that Wrightsville's history is being one of the "all-Black towns." She replied, "We had grocery stores. You could buy—filling stations. [I]t was . . . more of a town than it is now, let me say that." As I probed for the time period that she was talking about, she replied, "I want to say it was until over in the late, probably the late sixties, and I'm not really sure about that but I'll say the sixties. . . . We had . . . right there where the city hall is, that was a grocery store. . . . Then [another former resident] I think she opened up a café and a kind of dance hall there. Oh, and we had a barbershop there on the street." She considers Wrightsville to have been a "real town" when it had businesses. Her narrative equating businesses with a town that has life resonates with the narrative of Booker T. Washington and others who stamped Black towns as remarkable and energetic based on the same material qualities. Mrs. Jessup and others like her who can give an accounting of businesses in the town into the seventies keep alive the Black-town-history story of entrepreneurship and Black-community success in the past. In fact, they keep it alive about four decades longer than most official Black-town-history stories.

School Memories of Success in Loss

I always began my interviews by asking how people or their parents came to live in Black towns. The question seemed a good ice breaker and also a familiar one as people expected that town origins were my focus. Mrs. Jessup was receptive and explained that both her parents came to Wrightsville, separately, to attend Wrightsville's high school, which had a good reputation among rural Blacks. Her parents met there. Her father was from another, smaller Oklahoma Black town and traveled to the high school; her mother was from a racially "mixed" Oklahoma town, with a mostly German population,[17] and her family moved to Wrightsville. Mrs. Jessup displayed her knowledge of town history by providing details about the who and what of Wrightsville's most well-known school, which was then a secondary school for adults. She focused on a man credited with the school's origins:

> It was a man that was, uh, had been in the military. He ran the laundry . . . in town . . . and they drafted [him] in the military to run the laundry down there. . . . When he got out, uh, he started teaching at the school, elementary school. They felt that he should

have a job here 'cause when he left. . . . They were running a grocery store and his wife kept that store open while he was . . . was in the military. So, uh, the, the citizens and the board members decided that—. They felt that he should have a job at the school so they hired him to teach, and he was teaching the seventh and eighth graders. And, uh, he got—. The, the guys from World War II was coming in, young men, and he got involved in getting the high school out here in town 'cause he felt that the young men coming back from war, and with so many young ladies, you know, about their age range or younger, uh, it wasn't a good experience, you know. So . . . they moved the high school out here in the community. That's what happened.

Since the man's entrepreneur status enticed town leaders to find a role for him, the upshot is that businesses were central to Wrightsville. But, according to this story, so was education. Not only did the town leaders think it was important to accommodate the educational needs of an older Black male population; people from rural areas in this region of Oklahoma, including Mrs. Jessup's father, flocked to Wrightsville to advance their education through the school run by the returning veteran. As a Black educational focal point, Wrightsville was a place with status. The school provided an opportunity in a context of limited educational resources for rural Black youth, as Mrs. Jessup explained:

See, it was a lot of rural people and the rural kids and the people came and then people all over the state. There wasn't too many high schools in the state for Black people to go to. So, . . . just like my dad and there was another lady. . . . They were family friends 'til they passed, but she rode the train . . . with my dad, so both of them could come to school. You see what I'm talking about? And they were from the Green Valley area. And I know a lady still live here and she was from, uh, Newtown. She, that's how she got in Wrightsville and settled after she, she w-, came to high school, and then she got married, and then she bought, she and her husband bought property and they settled here.

The school Mrs. Jessup described later became Wrightsville Vocational School. Among Black towns in Oklahoma, Wrightsville stands out as a place that afforded status not just to the town but to Blacks across the state who attended the school at a time with few postsecondary options. I met dozens of people who either went to or were striving to attend Wrightsville Vocational. As one ninety-year-old Wrightsvillian told me, "Everybody wanted to come to Wrightsville because . . . being among [educated] people was good." In fact, unlike the case in other Black towns, many Wrightsville residents were not born and raised there. Many came to attend the vocational school or to work at it. Some never left.

Yet, although Wrightsville was distinct for its educational institution, all of Oklahoma's Black towns revere their schools—no matter the level. They consider the schools emblems of independence, social achievement, and unity. This, of course, reflects the value of education that Black communities have long attached to their prospects for mobility. Researching post-Emancipation, rural North Carolina, Vanessa Siddle Walker showed that a one-room segregated school served as the community's focal point.[18] Adults invested in the betterment of the community's children, even if the school resources—physical and educational—appeared bleak. Across the South, after Emancipation, Blacks sought out a variety of federal, state, and community resources to help build schools to educate their young. Despite conditions forcing Blacks to have separate schools that were underfunded and poorly resourced compared to White schools, Black communities rallied to make sure their communities had resources for education.[19]

Like Wrightsville, **Boley** has a prominent school narrative: the longevity of its primary and secondary schools. When I first went to Oklahoma in 2004, **Boley** was the only Black town that maintained active schools for its youth. All the other towns had "lost" their schools; the Black-town schools to serve Black youth had been forced to close their doors and integrate with neighboring White schools, usually due to population decline and unavailable resources to keep schools funded. In 2007, I heard much chatter about the fact that **Boley** was closing its high school, but, I often heard, "at least they are keeping their elementary school." From the town leadership, I sensed commitment to keeping the school open with its thirty-plus students in K–6. However, three years later the elementary school also closed, citing the loss of students to other schools and an inability to retain a school with such a small student body. The closing of **Boley's** elementary school signaled the end of Oklahoma's Black-town schools altogether. About this, in 2015, Mayor Shelton of **Boley** was quoted in a newspaper article on the endangerment of Black-town history as saying, "When you lose your school you lose your basis for being almost."[20] The mayor seemed to be commenting not about an individual's basis for being but about the community's.

Schools helped Black towns achieve their identity as spaces for Black independence and social status. In the 1970s, sociologist Charles A. Humphrey found that Black townspeople said the second most important "good feature" of their community was the schools (the first was good neighbors). Humphrey said, "[Schools] have been more than a center to educate the young; they have been focal points for social and political activities as well."[21] It isn't surprising, then, that among the people I talked to, they—like Mayor Shelton—expressed that losing their town school meant losing a signature piece of Black-town identity. Many contemporary events have been organized around revering and remembering the lost Black-town schools—this is a way to reconvene the community around one of its central features, even if that feature is a thing of the past.

Lima is one of a few Oklahoma Black towns with a standing Rosenwald School. During the first three decades of the twentieth century, more than five thousand such schools were funded by Sears and Roebuck founder Julius Rosenwald, who joined forces with Booker T. Washington to support the education of Black youth across the country.[22] Newtown and Promise had Rosenwald schools, as did some of their satellite communities, but their Rosenwald School buildings no longer exist. At the time of my research, **Lima's** school, like most school buildings that still stand in Black towns, was in utter disrepair. It had not been used as a school since the 1940s. That was when **Lima** consolidated with "New Lima," a neighboring White community that formed when Whites moved in after oil was "discovered" on town lands.[23] That consolidation still seemed a sore point when I spoke with some residents of **Lima** who were intent on renovating and repurposing the **Lima** school that had not been open for years.

In 2004, the town held a fundraiser for a political candidate who town leaders hoped would invest in their town and help support a project to remodel the school into a community center. Mayors from other Black towns also showed up for the big event, revealing how significant this gathering was for **Lima** but also for the Black-town community. We assembled under an outside tent in the evening with hanging lights connected to electricity from a nearby church. The lights flickered on and off throughout the event, stalling the activity a number of times. But the politician's speech was considered a success because he declared his support of **Lima**, making some town leaders beam throughout the night. The next day a longtime resident of **Lima** walked me over to the crumbling stone building to explain both her disappointment that the school stood in such disrepair and her vision for it to be

Abandoned school building in an Oklahoma Black town. Photo by author.

renovated. Its historic importance in the community, its status as one of the few Rosenwald Schools in the state, among Oklahoma Black towns, were her reasons for wanting it to be revived. She was sure that renovating the school would be a boost for **Lima**.

A deteriorated historic school, like the one in **Lima**, is a common image in Black towns. Even the Wrightsville Vocational School that Mrs. Jessup spoke about is an abandoned building, appearing to have suffered a fire. Almost all remaining Black towns have on their soils a building that is prominently placed—up on a hill, in the center of town—and yet also an eyesore because of its dilapidated condition. Most schools have broken-out windows, evidence of birds and other animals living inside, and are surrounded by weeds, sometimes waist-high. Some, like the one in Wrightsville, are half-burned by fire, but most have deteriorated from nonuse, closed after waves of outmigration, slimming financial resources, and the pressures of school desegregation made it harder for Black-town schools to hang on. The solution in all cases where the towns remained was for Black-town children to be sent to schools in neighboring, predominantly White towns, especially after desegregation in the 1950s.

The unused or no-longer-active buildings stand like holes that are felt in the communities. Time after time people described to us the era of school closings and the shift of Black-town youth to White-town schools as a dark period in Black-town history. It was an emotional experience, not merely because the schools provided an anchor and a sign of the town's independence. It was emotional because the shift to White schools was, for some, wrought with intense racial hostility. Priscilla Dunlap kept skirting direct questions about why she left Promise once Cromwell School, Promise's high school, closed. She explained that she went to Tulsa and never came back until she was an adult. She kept the details of her decision to leave Promise quite vague, almost like people who struggled to tell their family stories of unspeakable terror in the Deep South:

> PD: [I] did my last year at Booker T. [in Tulsa]. . . . Because I didn't want to go to the school down there in Pineway [a predominantly White town neighboring Promise]. It was—that was during that time and it was hard times. And they would write all kinda, the n-words all over our lockers and—do things, you know, and try to keep, try to make us, the Blacks, —do something, — . . . You know you gonna retaliate. And you know you're a teenage person. So, I just went on to Tulsa . . . rather than be in all of that, you know. I wasn't thinking about the [Civil Rights] movement. I wasn't thinking about that. It's not where my mind was, —you know, when all that [laughs], when all that stuff come up.
>
> KS: So you moved to Tulsa your senior year in high school. . . . Did your family go with you or—you went by yourself?
>
> PD: I went by myself. . . . Well I had other family up there in Tulsa. . . . And Booker T. was the Black high school at the time—. My sister, my oldest sister . . . come outta Promise. [Laughs]. . . . I went over and stayed with her—during that time—I stayed in Tulsa, got married. I came back home for a minute, about a year or so.

While some like Priscilla Dunlap opted to leave their town with the advent of integration, others who stayed recounted the struggles of that experience. Some said their education was much easier at White-town schools. It was easy in part because, as Mrs. Jessup pointed out, Black-town schools were rigorous. Or it was easy because Black youth were overlooked in the predominantly White schools where they ended up because White teachers didn't pay them any attention. "Sometimes we just sat back," a Wrightsvillian told me as he leaned back in his chair to demonstrate that he could "check out" of learning once he went to a neighboring White school. He laughed as he made the gesture, but it was clear that "checking out" or easy learning associated with a transition to White schools wasn't anything to celebrate.

Yet, the emotional devastation of losing Black-town schools reveals the appeal of the historical *presence* of schools for Black-town identity. The sense of loss is tied to what the presence meant. The history of Black towns, as told by elders who lived through the period of having Black-town schools and then losing them, hinges on the primacy of schools as institutional stalwarts in the communities. What happened when schools were lost—the physical and emotional devastation—is a narrative that people tell in a way that reveals how important the schools *were* and the void they left. Despair about their loss marked an acknowledgment that the Black-town school was a draw for Blacks in the community.

In Promise, Cromwell School was revered by many. Today it sits off in the distance from the town center, and you have to look for it. The lone building on a hill, it is surrounded by a field full of high weeds and, with its hollowed-out windows, looks deserted. Mr. Blanks was the force behind corralling former graduates to form a reunion, even though the school was no longer. Talking about his work on the reunion, we sat at his dining room table in a large house that he occupied on his own, his wife having passed away. He returned to Promise after retirement, but while he was away—living and working in Kansas City—he started mobilizing alumni from his generation to rally around Cromwell by returning for a homecoming.

Reunions are a big deal in Black towns, and almost every town has one, annually or biannually. They are not only a chance for people to reconnect; for these high-migration communities they are especially a time when people who have moved away come back to visit the town that they call home. Mr. Blanks took the lead in planning Cromwell's reunion. As he told the story:

In [the] latter part of 1960 I was very fond of Promise, and that's when I came back and I organized the Promise/Cromwell homecoming. . . . I started working on it in . . .'69, and we had our first homecoming in '71. . . . It . . . took about two years, and, and there were people, all these people that . . . was members of that organization that lived and attended high school here in Promise. . . . And I set up chapters. . . . There was a chapter in Wichita, there was a chapter in Tulsa, . . . in Kansas City, . . . and there was a chapter in Oakland.

So I had good cooperation. . . . It was . . . a wonderful, very wonderful gathering. . . . And people came from all over. . . . That's one of the . . . best things that ever happened here in Promise. . . . I mean people would come from . . . everywhere. . . . And . . . we had it—. Well, let's see. We had it in '71, '77, and '95.

He went on for several minutes telling me about the number of chapters and people who were involved in the school homecoming. Listening to him, it was clear that the school is the pride of the community and what people rally around. It stands as an important piece of the town's history. It may be a hollowed-out building that sits off in a distant, now-barren field. Yet the school unites because of its history as a force in the community and people's ability to remember the days they spent there, cultivated by Black educators. They don't rally around Civil Rights movements, as Priscilla Dunlap said. They rally around a structure in their community that kept them together. Telling the history of that school—before it closed—and drawing together the Black residents who attended the school during its heyday reinforces the memory of that bond. It also keeps alive the narrative of Black-town success and community.

Remembering Trauma and Success

In her well-known TED Talk, Chimamanda Ngozi Adichie discusses the "Danger of a Single Story," an account that only tells partial truths about a group of people.[24] Adichie focuses on stereotypes—the stories we as Americans tell ourselves and one another—that place Nigerians like her as other kinds of people; separate, unequal, and primitive. A single story leaves out Nigerians' humanity, complexity, and modernity.

Telling and profiling Black-town histories as triumphs allows for an attractive Black success story, but the story is not complete. The success story not only does the opposite of stripping Black people of their humanity but also limits understanding of their struggles with structural racism. Publicly profiling how Black people built economically engaged and socially inclusive communities might, on the one hand, appeal to a Black consumer who is drawn to a narrative that vindicates Blacks as deficient and without agency. On the other hand, downplaying histories of Black trauma can promote forgetting or ignoring Black struggles.

The Black-town story that incorporates traumatic beginnings is more complex and includes remembering a variety of experiences. It positions the

Black town as an appealing place because it is understood as a place of refuge and Black agency. When elders told us about their families' Southern traumas that sparked their families' movement to join Western Black towns, the stories highlighted not merely a will and energy to be socially mobile. They also highlighted a response to extreme racism, rooting the appeal of a Black town in its answer to life-threatening events. After this, some of those narratives detail Blacks' material and social success—through gaining property in a Black town—*after* overcoming racism. That the stories also return to trauma in the moment of school integration bookends the narrative with trauma and loss. But telling the story of school loss is also a way to remember Black-town success by underscoring memories of successful schooling and education that served as an anchor for the community. Thus, success stories of the material and social conditions that attracted Black people to Black towns or made them fond of the places are mixed with accounts of terror and loss. Residents' stories of Black-town history, then, are complex, stitching trauma in a narrative of success that admits challenges and triumphs without considering the former a marker of Black-town demise or insignificance.

Attempts to pin up Black success as a community feature contend with the institutions that terrorized people, including legalized segregation, integration, and White supremacy. Yet, as they engage with this part of Black-town history, Black-town residents can rally around moments and memories of success. The stories they tell that highlight Black achievement and progress are profiled even if, when told, some of those stories acknowledge struggle, terror, and disappointment. Still, even in the stories of loss and terror, Black towns are remembered and narrated as appealing spaces of refuge, where material and social success wasn't always linear but was achieved at different moments.

CHAPTER TWO

The Case for America

The Greyhound bus swayed slightly back and forth as we drove down the dirt road leading to Green Valley, the second stop on a tour of Black towns sponsored by the Black Heritage Society of Tulsa, Oklahoma. We merged onto Interstate 40, picked up speed, and headed for the tour's final stop, in Oklahoma City. There, we spent four hours touring the Oklahoma City National Memorial and Museum, which commemorates the 1995 bombing of the city's federal building. We also toured exhibits at the Oklahoma History Center, which its website says is devoted to "exploring Oklahoma's unique history of geology, transportation, commerce, culture, aviation, heritage and more."[1] The contrast between our visits to Green Valley (the only recognized Black town on this particular tour) and Oklahoma City was striking. In Green Valley, where we toured for thirty-five minutes, we stayed on the bus and were greeted by Ben Walker, a resident who stood in the bus aisle while pointing out the town's buildings, including grocery stores, pool halls, and railroad station. His listing of town establishments was in keeping with a typical rundown of town businesses others use to tell Black-town successful histories. At the Oklahoma History Center, we went on self-guided tours of exhibits about Black history in the state (the exhibits included some Black-town history but also much else). At the memorial, we also walked on our own through the indoor and outdoor portions of the site, for what turned out to be our longest tour stop of the day. The tour of Green Valley, a designated Black town, was far surpassed in time and breadth by the museum tours in Oklahoma City, a city never designated as a Black town in any official material.

The first Black Heritage Society tours of Black towns that began in the late 1990s only visited physical, conventionally recognized Black towns—that is, one of the thirteen remaining towns. Some tours today, and during the time of my research, do indeed include the recognized towns, and visits to them can make up a greater proportion of the total stops. Yet for the tours I frequented between 2006 and 2009, Black-town tourist itineraries included visits to sites that represent neither the officially recognized physical space of Black towns nor spaces obviously linked to Black towns. Indeed, although there were Blacks who perished in the 1995 bombing, the memorial has no noted significance to Black towns, Blacks in Oklahoma, or Black people in general. It was also not unusual for tour stops at nonobvious Black-town sites to supersede (in time and narration) visits to the thirteen recognized Black towns. What I observed, then, is that Black-town tours were sometimes dislocated from the "official" towns' physicality, and tour narration expanded beyond the past or present life within Black towns geographically proper. Given this, you might imagine disgruntled tourists, wondering if they were victims of false advertisement and also curious why a Black-town tour did not stick to Black towns. And yet, I found that the tours were quite popular, and the tourists I interviewed all raved about their experience. What is the attraction to these unofficial Black-town sites on a Black-town tourism event?

Space, Time, Heritage

Analysis of the tour narratives and structure might give us some clues. Although not mentioned anywhere in the written or spoken tour narrative, the bombing memorial is a site of violence reminiscent of the unspeakable terror that prompted Black-town formation. Terrorist violence is also familiar to Black residents of Tulsa, who are frequent participants in some Black-town tours I went on and who know all about the destruction of Greenwood, the Black business area in Tulsa that was decimated by White violence in 1921. Thus, the structure of some tours that went to Oklahoma City engaged the theme of White violence that connects the memorial, Black towns, and Black Tulsa, even if those connections were implicit and not explicitly unpacked by a tour narrator.

Beyond this, we must also situate tours of Black towns within the broader realm of heritage tours because organized tourist events to Black towns explore sites and peoples deemed to be "historically significant."[2] Some argue that, even while trading on an idea of historical significance, heritage tourism relies on discourses and politics of the present to narrate the past.[3] Narratives of the past are a performance or cultural production of the present cloaked in historical analysis. This occurs when tourists are guided to make sense of a particular historical event or historically significant group or region through an implicit fluidity of time. Particular sites or groups are read through significant and suggested reference to a time period other than the one openly profiled in the tour event itself, sometimes to connect with the current perspectives or concerns of a specific audience.[4] Heritage is presented through meanings of the present, appealing to contemporary consumers.[5] Put simply, "then" is viewed through "now."

Indeed, although the terrorizing of Tulsa's Greenwood neighborhood was eighty years before the Black-town tour to the bombing memorial, the tour occurred just a few years after public awareness and discussion of Greenwood's history with racial violence expanded amid formal state recognition of the event that leveled the community. Around this time, a number of publications, movies, and events devoted to exploring that past circulated actively in Oklahoma. Greenwood's destruction, therefore, had significant present-day currency that factored into how a Black-town bus tourist might interpret a visit to the memorial.

There is also a spatial dimension through which heritage tours tell a particular story. Discussing 1990s tourism in New Orleans, American Studies scholar Lynell Thomas observes how a tour narrative that was intended to highlight New Orleans as a "multicultural city" but involved effacing Black culture as tourist activities were removed from the city's spaces where Black resistance and survival had taken place. Tourism was spatially designed and linked to unexpected sites to limit the inclusion of blackness in the tour, making it more palatable for tourist sensibilities.[6] Indeed, the meanings tours seek to convey rely on specific uses of space, but the spatial shifting of tours outside expected and conventional boundaries of place is less common. Most heritage tours in the country and around the world are fairly fixed in place. They involve a visit to the actual location where an event occurred, an individual lived, a community existed. I once went on a tour of South Africa's Robben Island, where Nelson Mandela was imprisoned, and we were confined to the island and the prison buildings on it. Tours of "Black Wall Street" in Durham, North Carolina, stay around Parrish Street, where the district's Black-run finance buildings and businesses were located. The tours might go to neighboring Hayti, a residential and commercial area, but Hayti was integrated with Black economic life on Parrish Street. The tours do not go to the state history museum in Raleigh or to Durham's Stagville plantation, ten miles away. Tour narrators might talk about connections with other, more distant sites but would not typically claim other physical spaces as part of the designated heritage site in question. Thus, by going to places like the Oklahoma History Center, Black-town tours are atypical in their spatial breadth even if the ways that they play with time are familiar across tours of other sites.

That Black Heritage Society tours rely on a geographically unfixed notion of the Black-town mirrors what geographers and other scholars have told us. Boundaries of place are constructed, fluid, and variable.[7] Places and spaces are mobile and engaged in networks, flows that transcend local and national boundaries.[8] In his influential book *Harlemworld*, John L. Jackson showed us how spatial fluidity works in a Black place when he detailed how Black residents in New York's Harlem anchor themselves in the neighborhood for its significance as a Black cultural mecca. All the while, they actively maintain social ties across multiple and diverse areas of the city beyond Harlem, thereby engaging their complex class and race identities.[9] For Black Heritage Society tours as well as some other tourist events focused on Black towns, by situating the towns in unconventional and expansive spatial contexts, the events achieve what temporal shifting of other heritage tours achieves. That is to say, they cross and connect different spaces that have a specific and salient meaning at a particular moment to a particular group. For tours of Black towns that especially cater to African Americans, that meaning concerns themes around race, especially race relations, racial injustice, and racial origins at the foundations of the country. In short, the tours offer a narrative about race in America. They do so not merely by discussing what happened one hundred years ago in thirteen small, racially identified towns in Oklahoma. They talk about race in America by analytically, symbolically, and physically linking Black towns to a range of American spaces, places, and landmarks. Those spaces and places have symbolic or overt racial meanings, but they also hold meaning as emblems of America. Connecting Black people to these spaces and fixtures, tour narrators are able to unpack American dialogues on race and the place of African Americans in the country. The tour design remakes space and redefines Black towns,[10] lifting the towns out of remoteness and connecting them more directly with themes and discourses that are centrally about America, sometimes in contested ways. Moreover, the fluidity of space and time demonstrated on tours of Black towns enables a larger argument about the placement of Black towns, an argument about the central relevance and location of Black towns. Because the spatial and temporal breadths of tours place Black towns ubiquitously, the tour narrative presents a claim about Blacks' rightful place in the country. What is alluring about the tour, then, is its ability to detail successful Black histories but also to leverage an *appeal*—a case—for Black worth centrally and expansively in the nation.

As tour narrators reposition Black towns from their remote physical and temporal location to more prominent and ubiquitous sites and times resonating with the major themes of the country, they situate Black towns as essentially American places with ties to American centers of modernity. For tour consumers, Black towns go from the common pre-tour assumption that the towns are historically important and contemporarily remote and marginal, to the post-tour understanding that the towns have major ties to—if not major original responsibility for—people, places, and events that are at the origins of American society *today*. Moreover, tour consumers leave tours understanding that Black towns are situated in America's quintessential social, political, and economic moments and discourses. This becomes an understanding and commentary about bringing Black Americans out of marginality into American centers. Tour narratives elevate Black towns in a way that is especially meaningful for Black American tourists in general and Oklahoma Black Americans in particular. The result of the tour is an understanding of Black towns that have an American appeal.

The Tour in Context

To gain this understanding, on Black Heritage Tours tourists can participate in any of the several different tours operated in Oklahoma. All originate in urban areas. Most got their start in the late 1990s, although new tours have been added as recently as 2015. Most tours are also publicly funded through municipalities or the state. They range from biannual summer tours that bring close to one hundred bus tourists in a given year to visit different Black-town sites across the state, to special-occasion theme tours held for visiting groups, such as conference attendees, to small commissioned tours organized at the request of individual tourists.

The Black Heritage Society's tours occur twice annually and began in the late 1990s as a joint venture between two community organizations serving a predominantly Black area of Tulsa, one of them devoted to "protecting [and] preserving . . . African American history and culture" and the other focused on correcting the historical record regarding Blacks in Oklahoma and Tulsa in particular. According to tour coordinators, Black Heritage Society tour routes are determined by whether towns can accommodate large buses or groups. Other factors include the town's fame, the abundance of its historic resources, and its proximity to the tour starting place. Certain towns are common staples in tours of Black towns: **Boley**, billed as one of the largest and most successful of the Black towns given its once commercial sector and infrastructural development; three or four towns in relative close proximity to Tulsa such as **Taft**, a Black town with historic social-service institutions for Black Americans; and **Rentiesville**, which sits on the border of a historic Civil War battlefield and is also the birthplace of renowned historian John Hope Franklin and home to the late blues icon DC Minner. Additionally, tours sometimes include **Langston**, also known for its historically active business development. Tours rarely stop at small towns with few visible historic buildings or landmarks. But common to many tours are stops at the Battle of Honey Springs, a Civil War landmark, and Fort Gibson Historic Site, a military post from the nineteenth century. Neither of these are officially designated Black towns, but they are sites where Black American soldiers were active.

Tulsa: A Native Black Town

In 2006, the Black Heritage Society sponsored a tour that included a stop in the Black town of **Rentiesville**, but, as with the tour to Green Valley, the rest of the tour was focused elsewhere. This tour was billed as a tour of Black cemeteries and churches. On one prior occasion the tour included "Black towns and landmarks," when it profiled a site where Buffalo Soldiers—African American soldiers who were part of the U.S. Army regiment in the West during the mid-nineteenth century—lived and fought. With the focus on churches and cemeteries, the tour shifted the conventional definition of "All Black Towns." Rather than looking to towns' racial composition as the point of definition, towns and other localities became read as Black towns once tour narrators could link churches and cemeteries to Black American founders. Designating sites with landmarks relevant to Black history as Black towns meant that Tulsa—the second-largest city in the state—could be included *as a Black town*. This is because the tour focused on a particular cemetery in the city that one of the tour's narrators, Allen, identified as having deep significance for Blacks in the city and state.

For several years, Allen was a tour historian on other Black Heritage Society tours of Black towns. He was part of the original planning of the tour and, as the tour booklet explained, he is a historian by training and provided the initial maps and "historical content for the [first-ever bus] tours." One of the tour's staff members told me that they believed Allen[11] actually came up with the idea for the Black-town tours. In addition to the tour to Green Valley and Oklahoma City, he also narrated a tour focused on Tulsa that I participated in. For that tour, I was sitting in the front of the bus, where a tour staff member, who knew that I was writing a book about Black towns, had strategically placed me, emphasizing that Allen had a lot of good knowledge that I should capture. Others who I talked to later also expressed delight with his historical insight, which they felt was, in part, shaped by his long-term residence in Oklahoma. "He is an encyclopedia," one Tulsa resident and tourist told me.

From where I was perched, Allen stood directly in front of me, holding a microphone as he stood in the bus stairwell. The videographer, there to visually document the event and who was instructed to get everything Allen said, sat next to me. We bumped elbows a lot as he tried to position the large video camera so he could record Allen and as I was writing feverishly, my arm flopping about as I, too, attempted to catch every one of Allen's words. "Although this is a Black-town tour," Allen said, "we are going to put the cart before the horse. . . . We are going to show you some of Tulsa's best-kept secrets." With this reference to Tulsa, Allen began immediately reconstructing definitions of Black towns by indicating that this major Oklahoma city would be featured in a tour of Black towns. He went on to say that Black towns in Oklahoma are divided into "State" or "Native" towns. Native towns, he explained, were those formed by Africans who came to the Americas before Europeans, while State towns were organized and delineated by the state through the Congressional Dawes Act. That is, for Allen, Native towns were formed by pre-Colombian-era Africans settling in what became known as Indian territory; State towns grew out of the federal reassignment of Oklahoma territory—although, importantly, Allen never specified such reassignment.

It is precisely the concept of "Native towns"—as pre-Columbian towns founded by Africans—that sets Allen's Black-town history apart from the histories told by others. Historians indeed delineate "Native Blacks" and "State Blacks" (called "State Negroes" at the time) in Oklahoma history, the former being Freedmen and the latter being people who migrated from the South.[12] Native towns are those formed by Freedmen, African descendants formerly enslaved by American Indians. Allen critiqued this historical account and its ideas about how Blacks came to Oklahoma when he exclaimed, "It is a myth that Indians came with slaves! [People] have you believing that Indians came with all these slaves. Indians came with no slaves. [Only] a few misfits dealt in slaves." Indeed, he went further to explain that those we consider "Natives" were not Indians at all, but actually of African origin. Thus, for him, Tulsa was a Black town formed by Africans who settled the place before European arrival on the continent.

TO BOLSTER THIS POINT, he offered a critique of "the whole Bering Strait theory," the theory (also known as the Bering Strait Land-Bridge Theory) of original human migration to the Americas across land from Asia, which he claimed false. This put Allen in the company of other critics of the theory who question who first came to America and how. One such critic is the late

African American anthropologist Ivan Van Sertima who, more than forty years ago, in his book *They Came before Columbus: The African Presence in Ancient America*, offered the then provocative but widely read argument of a pre-Columbian African presence in the Americas dating back to the seventh century.[13] For Van Sertima, Africans were pioneer explorers and settlers of the region, evidenced by artifacts showing an African imprint.[14] Another challenger to the Bering Strait thesis is Native American author, academic, and activist Vine Deloria. In *Red Earth, White Lies: Native Americans and the Myth of Scientific Fact*, published two decades after Van Sertima's book, Deloria also challenged the Bering Strait theory of migration and questioned the veracity of archaeological evidence used to explain how ancestors of American Indians arrived in the Americas.[15] While other critics of the Bering Strait theory exist and still challenge the argument, especially for ignoring Native American cultural beliefs about their origins in North America,[16] both Deloria and Van Sertima attracted especially strong popular followings along with academic criticism of their arguments. Allen did not mention Deloria, Van Sertima, nor any of these other critics. Still, he seemed steeped in their ideas when developing his own unconventional argument on Black origins in Oklahoma, which he shared with the nonacademic audience on the bus.

By claiming that "we" are mistaking Africans for Native Americans when we think about who was original to America, Allen was also arguing for an early African presence that preceded not only Europeans but also American Indians. When he made this claim, he did not say much to explain *why* we are mistaken, but later in the tour, perhaps, he offered some proof when he pointed out mounds on the side of a country road, almost an hour outside Tulsa. The mounds, he said, are labeled by archaeologists as Native American mounds, but are actually filled with artifacts from Africans and, therefore, they are evidence of early African presence. Such evidence would point to Africans being first in the Americas — not as chattel or second-class citizens, but as innovators of the earliest *civilized* cultures.

This emphasis on "Native" status has deep significance in the Oklahoma context of Black and Indian relations.[17] Again, the term "Native" has been used to differentiate Blacks hierarchically, dividing those who migrated to Oklahoma from the U.S. South (non-Natives) and those who were Freedmen. "Native," a higher status than non-Native, was reserved for the Freedmen who considered themselves to be "original" in Oklahoma Territory (or more original than those who migrated from the South). Moreover, the pejorative Creek word for non-Native meant both "White person" and "intruder."[18] And even more recently, some note that the higher social status often assigned to "Freedmen natives"—for being more original to the region—carried over and was still a source of tension in Black towns at least through the end of the twentieth century.[19] But Allen offered no such differentiation between Freedmen and Black Southern migrants as he collapsed Blacks in the state into one group: natives. The implication of his discussion was that all Blacks were native and no Blacks intruded; they originally settled Oklahoma, not *after* Native Americans relocated to what is now Oklahoma but *as* Native Americans.

Allen's mention of the mounds and his claims about African "Natives" bolstered the analytical work he had already done much more forcefully and extensively when he interpreted Tulsa as a Native Black town. He achieved this reading through a lengthy discussion and analysis of the Perryman family, known as one of the significant business-owning and founding Indian families in the city. By his account (and reinforced by the collective "uh huh" of the bus-tour participants), the Perrymans are viewed as a "wealthy, wealthy family" and an "original family of Tulsa." Allen said this after he told tourists they were about to see "Tulsa's best-kept secrets," and as the bus pulled up to the first stop at Utica and 32nd Avenue in Midtown Tulsa, approximately fifteen minutes from the bus's start in the Black community of North Tulsa. It is also the site of Tulsa's oldest cemetery, which contains plots for members of the Perryman family. Indeed, it is called the Perryman Cemetery and sits in the middle of a residential block, gated off by a tall iron fence. The surrounding neighborhood featured manicured lawns, driveways with multiple vehicles (often SUVs and four-door sedans), and a tennis court. Located within the city limits of Tulsa, the area had a very suburban feel quite distinct from that of North Tulsa, where residences sit alongside businesses, a historically Black university, and a then-lifeless downtown. The streets of North Tulsa, even at 7:30 A.M., when the bus tour began, are beginning to move with traffic. But by 8:00 A.M. in Midtown Tulsa, there were no moving vehicles (except the tour bus). Compared to the activity in North Tulsa, the quiet in the neighborhood was striking—a quiet that, symbolically, the tour was there to disturb.

Walking among headstones in the cemetery, where bus tourists noticed numerous references to Perryman family members, Allen talked about the cemetery and its significance to Blacks. Although he did not say much about Perryman family history, he emphasized that most people do not think of the Perrymans as Black. Indeed, the Perryman family is renowned. Lewis

Perryman is the family patriarch, credited with being Tulsa's founder and identified widely as being Creek Indian. However, Allen announced that the Perryman family members are Black, and their racial identity is a history and ancestry that most accounts deny. His argument that the Perryman family members have African ancestry is borne out in literature.[20] It is also supported in the *Power of Place* exhibit at the National Museum of African American History and Culture (NMAAHC), which refers to the Perrymans as both a "founding family" of Tulsa and a "mixed-race" family, including White, Creek, and African American members.[21] Allen mentioned that many Perryman men married African American women, implying that Perryman offspring would be Black as a result. However, his argument was also that, given African origins in the Americas, the Perrymans who were "original" to Oklahoma were necessarily African in ancestry. Allen's critique of the Bering Strait theory, presumably, was his justification for such a claim. He did not explicitly say this. However, he concluded the stop at the cemetery by saying, "This is why we want to show you . . . [Tulsa] is a native Black town."

At the same time, although Allen never mentioned the Perrymans' perceived race (he talked more about what he believed they are rather than what they are not), the plaque at the entrance of the cemetery described the family as Creek. It identified the Perryman patriarch, Lewis, as "one of the most prominent ranchers and traders in the Creek Nation." Across encyclopedia entries and historical accounts of Tulsa and the Perryman family there are many other references to the Perrymans as a Creek family. But there are other references, such as the one at the NMAAHC, that raise questions about the singularity of that identity for the family. A Black Historical Society staff member showed me another reference in documents that Allen provided and that inspired the tour's focus on Tulsa. The documents included colonial-era U.S. government reports on the "Five Civilized Tribes" (the term for the American Indian tribes that were relocated to the West), entries from an online forum known as the African-Native American Genealogy Forum, and a series of write-ups (articles and captioned photographs) on the Perryman family. The thinking was that the documents contained information revealing the African influence and importance to the "Five Civilized Tribes"— especially the Creek Nation—and also the African origins of the Perryman family. The person showing me the documents pointed out two features: a sentence from a 1904 government report stating that the Creek were descendants of "the Yamassee," a group described as having immigrated from Africa, and a photograph of the Perryman family, in which, the person told me, Legus C. Perryman appeared to have Black phenotypic features. "This is explosive information," another staff member said, sounding as shocked as many of the bus tourists later would be as they roamed the cemetery listening to Allen's narration.

Yet, as Allen interpreted Tulsa for us as an original Black place and Native Black town because the founding family was Black, he did so in what appeared to be a White space—it certainly felt like that to the tourists. Some told me that they consider the neighborhood to be a "White area," and a few Black tourists said they were wholly unfamiliar with "that part of town." Some of Tulsa's most upscale markers are in Midtown: the highest-end shopping plazas known as Utica Square and Brookside; Woodland Park, known for its spring azalea blooms; Cherry Street district, a kind of Tulsa Soho; and the historic area of Mapleside, where oil executives live. While these are mostly economic indices, North Tulsa residents on the bus were clear that the prestige of the space suggested to them that it was not a Black area, and, to be sure, Allen appeared to play right into that perception. His racial reading of the Perrymans was achieved not simply through a statement and analysis of the family's blackness. His reading was also possible due to the space in which he analyzed the family. That is, as Allen transposed conventional understandings of the Perrymans to expose their Black origins, he was able to flip their identity not merely by his words but also by his use of the space. If the tour was meant to reveal hidden secrets, the revelation of a founding Black family situated—unbeknownst to the public—in an elite White space would do the trick. While remaking the Perryman identity, Allen provided a shocking piece of information that Black bus tourists latched onto, in part because of the racial meaning of the space in which that identity shift was made.

The larger state context matters, too, as Oklahomans are well familiar with a view that Indians in the state—those who belong to the "Five Civilized Tribes" believed to have "assimilated" to European lifestyles (often by force) and intermarried with Whites—may appear "phenotypically White." Thus, for the tourists, transforming the Perrymans' racial identity from Indian to Black in a White neighborhood allowed them to infer that the prominence of that Indian identity was shaped by its connection to White identity and spaces in Oklahoma. In the end, tourists walked away with an understanding that a major Oklahoma city that they believed to be founded by partially White-identified American Indians living in urban spaces, which they considered off-limits to Blacks, was actually a Black town pioneered by people with African origins, like many of those on the bus.

The Blackness of Black-Town Tours

Despite Allen's layering of Black identities with Whiteness and Native/Indianness to make a point about Black people's prominence in the state and country, the tour was also centered firmly in blackness. This is because, in many ways, the tours are about American blackness just like organized tours of historic sites in West Africa are pitched to African Americans, playing into desires for diasporic connections and exploration of roots.[22] Directly or indirectly, such tours of Black towns touch on Black people, places, and experiences not always clearly tied to Black towns. Tours of Black towns visit places and landmarks somehow indicative of "Black communities." They profile people who are famous Black figures in Oklahoma. They highlight sites known to have had Black American residents. Additionally, they connect with sites and figures that are not necessarily about Black Americans or Black Oklahomans but that can be, and often are, read through Black American experiences and sensibilities. By not being site specific, they engage widely with American blackness, often appealing to the perspective of Black tourists from anywhere in Oklahoma and sometimes from anywhere in the United States.

North Tulsa and the Racial Divide

When Allen analyzed Tulsa as a Black town, he did so for a predominantly African American audience resident in North Tulsa because, as mentioned previously, the tour out of Tulsa strives to serve that community. What is the North Tulsa community? Popularly, North Tulsa is recognized as *the* Black neighborhood of Tulsa given its history and demographics, although those demographics probably are not what most assume. In 2010, 16 percent of the City of Tulsa's population was identified as African American, compared to 41 percent of North Tulsa's population.[23] The Black population in North Tulsa represents 43 percent of the entire Black population in Tulsa County, a spatial concentration that has decreased over the past four decades since integration. Although North Tulsa has the highest concentration of Blacks in the county, more Blacks live outside North Tulsa than in it.[24] Over time, African Americans have spread out into other neighborhoods of the city and county where such movement previously was not possible. On the other hand, non-Blacks have also increasingly moved into North Tulsa. Indeed, in 2010, 30 percent of the community was made up of Whites, 18 percent were Latinx, and 5 percent were American Indians.[25] Thus, North Tulsa has become more racially diverse since the 1960s, as has the rest of Tulsa County and city. At the same time, how these groups are distributed within North Tulsa matters: the northwest area of North Tulsa, for instance, has a higher concentration of Whites, while the northernmost part of North Tulsa—known popularly as Deep North Tulsa—has the highest concentration of Blacks.

Demographic distribution notwithstanding, the widespread perception of North Tulsa as "the Black area" and perceptions about the spatial dimension of race and residence in the city matter significantly. Tulsans may not be able to rattle off what percentage of which racial group lives where, but they can tell you their ideas about the racial identity of a given area, even if there is some variation in those ideas. Bus tourists easily identified Midtown for me as a White area, and they were clear that North Tulsa is Black. Such perceptions played into how the bus-tour events were structured as well as how bus tourists interpreted the tour activities and content.

For example, Black Heritage Society tours had a very "community feel," as if participants on the bus were from a similar area and were familiar with the same community referents. Allen constantly began his sentences with "I know you all know . . ." and he would finish the sentence mentioning a building, business, or event that he presumed was familiar to those on the bus. His presumption often was confirmed with a chorus of "uh huhs" that felt like a call-and-response exchange. Similarly, when the bus stopped in Green Valley, many tourists asked Ben Walker, the resident who got on the bus to tell us about the town, if he knew a particular family. "Do you know the Simmons family?" a tourist called out, interrupting Mr. Walker's narration. Another followed: "Do you know Louie?" "Yes, I know Uncle Louie," Walker quickly replied, and everybody laughed. Bus tourists from North Tulsa likely knew these family names because, especially since the end of legalized segregation, people migrating out of Black towns to Tulsa often settled in North Tulsa. Members of the North Tulsa community, consequently, become familiar with key family names from places like **Taft**, **Redbird, Rentiesville, Tullahassee**, or **Summit**—the Black towns closest to Tulsa. Of course, the tour included many people who lived outside North Tulsa, but tour narration and interaction tended to assume North Tulsa as the shared Black experience on the bus. Indeed, the few White tourists whom I interviewed were struck more by the connections and camaraderie among Black bus tourists than they were by the tour content (in contrast to the vast majority of Black bus tourists being struck by the information about Black history that they learned on the tour). In short, the bus tour was largely a Black space.

Allen's take on the Perryman family is another clear example of how Tulsa's racial setup played into the tour. For Black Tulsan bus tourists—especially North Tulsa tourists—the visit to the Perryman sites stood out as the most impactful aspects of the tour. There was urgency, excitement, and passion in the voices of these tourists as they reacted to the information about the Perrymans. Many expressed surprise at learning that an area they had always assumed to be White and wealthy had not only Blacks living in it but notable Blacks responsible for the formation of the area and the entire city. Among tourists, there was less interest in the Perrymans as a specific family (some admitted never having heard the Perryman name) than in the idea of a prominent Black family located in Midtown Tulsa and being responsible for the creation of the city. A retired Black female tourist from North Tulsa who described herself as "staying in her corner" in the north part of the city expressed both shock and delight at the information. Telling me that she is unapologetic and steadfast in her view that Whites always take what is "rich and of value" from Blacks, she found the visit to the Perryman cemetery especially significant:

> I always enjoy the first part . . . the first stop, the cemetery. . . . To know that among all those multimillionaires . . . to know that there's a Black family. . . . I mean, it's just . . . I'm just . . . it's just amazing. It's so incredible. . . . My husband had been through this [area] because his first employer is a drapery installer. He was installing drapes in these multimillionaires' homes and they made him aware of [the area]. . . . But, when I drive through [on the tour] and to know that the Helmerich family, Helmerich and Payne Corporation [oil company], they live right . . . like, not far from there. And they [are] on Utica Square and the richest strip in Tulsa, Oklahoma. My relatives helped to raise his children as their maids and cooks. To think that Blacks are buried right in his back door. That's just . . . I just . . . it's absolutely incredible. But, we just never stopped to go [to that area] until the tour.

Like this tourist, others made it clear that they either had never been to the area where the Perryman cemetery is located or had passed through but never imagined it had anything to do with Blacks or their own experience. As the above tourist explained, "this" part of town was a far cry from "her corner" in the north. Midtown is the space where the social and economic gap between Tulsan Whites and Blacks stands out. The tour, then, appealed to her sense—as a North Tulsan—of the active social divisions in the city.

The tour also tapped into perceptions of Tulsa's racial-spatial gap that stems from memories and recently circulating information about the 1921 "race riot"—some say "massacre"—in North Tulsa. North Tulsa is perhaps best-known for its early twentieth-century Greenwood business district, sometimes referred to as "Black Wall Street." As with Black towns, North Tulsa boasted a wide array of Black-owned businesses and professional services available for African American residents in the area during the early 1900s.[26] Yet in 1921, Greenwood was razed following a lengthy period of intense racial violence that resulted in the destruction of the Black commercial district and many residential homes nearby. Enduring over two days, the events were sparked by erroneous claims that a Black man had assaulted a White woman in an elevator. In what followed, many Blacks in Greenwood were killed and had their businesses and homes burned down by angry Whites.[27] The neighborhood, once economically and socially vibrant, had to be rebuilt practically from scratch while residents lived in tent camps for months.

Although it was not until 1997 that a state government commission was formed to research what happened, the 1921 events in Greenwood have become the signature episode most associated with North Tulsa. The past decade has seen a spate of books, public lectures, film screenings on White violence and the destruction of Greenwood. There also have been public-recognition events, the creation of a John Hope Franklin Center for Reconciliation, an application to place Greenwood on the National Register of Historic Places, and attempts to establish reparations for the survivor families. Given this sudden (but overdue) and concentrated attention on Greenwood over a recent and relatively short period of time, North Tulsans—and Tulsans in general—have become accustomed to seeing the massacre in Greenwood as a defining historical feature of the community. Recognition and sustained discussion about historic violence to the Black community and its legacy have brought Tulsa's racial disparities into sharper relief and mobilized public consciousness, especially among Black Tulsans. What is more, many public activities recognizing the assault on Greenwood have been sponsored by the Black Heritage Society.

Not surprisingly then, the Black-town bus tours have contributed to the effort to raise awareness about the 1921 "riots." This is achieved especially by including on-bus lectures and videos about the racial violence and its impact on the North Tulsa community. Between tour stops, tour narrators commonly provide information about the destruction of Greenwood—either by telling of the events and their implications or by discussing them in relation to other issues (such as Black-town life). It is also safe to say that including Greenwood's destruction in the tour's narration sits well with or, in some cases, motivates tourists because of their knowledge of the events. Some tourists have family members who survived the violence against the Greenwood community. Others have researched the 1921 events on their own, or they attended events covering the community's history and destruction. Still others have been involved in the movement demanding reparations for survivors.

Given such sensibilities around the Greenwood devastation, it is understandable that most of the Black Tulsa bus participants talked about the suppression of Black history as a persistent and pervasive problem that needs correcting. Some mentioned the Greenwood events as an example, noting that the destruction of Greenwood is part of Oklahoma history that is not covered in schools. Some heard about Greenwood's history from family members who experienced the events or from other people who knew about them, either in North Tulsa or in larger African American circles. They felt that the community's decimation had not been publicly and officially discussed until very recently. Others drew a connection between the suppression of this specific North Tulsa history and the untold stories of the Black towns. Tourists discussed how Black towns, like the destruction of Greenwood, are neglected in history classes in Oklahoma public schools. They believe that the Black-town historical experience is a little-known but important part of American history that involves Blacks succeeding, surviving, and exhibiting independence. "All we ever hear about are Blacks as slaves," said one North Tulsa resident who had been on three tours and visited the Black towns on her own as well. "My goal [for taking the tour] is to teach children that we weren't only slaves, that *we had a lot to do with the making of America*" (emphasis mine). Others told me they either brought their children along or participated in the tour to be able to "widen the circle" (as one Tulsa resident put it) of information sharing and knowledge about the place of Black American histories in the state and country.

There was also another way the tour used the city of Tulsa to reveal patterns of race and inequality. This concerns the tribal membership status of Cherokee Freedmen, a debate that played out seventy miles south of Tulsa, where the Cherokee Nation is located. When creating tribal lists in the nineteenth century, the U.S. government distinguished tribal members based on whether they were "Freedmen" or "non-Freedmen," but both sets of individuals were given full tribal rights. This was even though, at the time, palpable social divisions between the two groups existed within most of the tribes. Tribes often excluded Freedmen from holding full tribal citizenship, attaining positions in tribal governments, or marrying or "mixing" with "full blood" tribe members.[28] Indeed, with the advent of the Dawes land allotments and the breaking up of tribal structures, many tribal members sought to leave Indian Territory (present-day Oklahoma), with Freedmen and non-Freedmen pursuing different avenues of escape based on a notion of nonshared identity.[29]

Yet, the shift in tribe status in the 1970s changed the possibilities for tribal membership. Under the Indian Self-Determination and Education Assistance Act of 1975 (and also after subsequent revisions to the act), tribal nations were reconstituted, granted greater self-governance, and became able to set up their own governments. They also could decide who had legal rights to tribal nation citizenship. In the case of some tribes, this led to tribal government decisions to exclude ancestors of Freedmen from tribal citizenship, based on blood, as determined by the Dawes Commission.[30] As anthropologist Circe Sturm describes regarding the Cherokee Nation, a 2007 vote to exclude "Non-Indians" (understood as Freedmen and "Inter-married Whites") cited the Dawes Commission tribal rolls as proof of Freedmen's non-Indianness — they were not on the rolls as being Indian "by blood."[31] Voters were told that allowing Freedmen to remain in the Cherokee Nation would mean including people who were not Indian and who would yet be entitled to services and resources of the nation. Legal disputes on this matter were active in Oklahoma, and some were especially pronounced in Tulsa and surrounds. This heated moment of political, economic, and social exclusion based on race and ancestral blood, as well as the public tensions and protracted debates regarding tribal membership, also form the backdrop to the 2006 tours' rereading of race and privilege in Tulsa. That is, just as the 1921 destruction of Greenwood was an early 2000s "hot topic" about racial inequality and White violence against Blacks in Tulsa, so too was the Cherokee Nation's ruling a prominent story with currency about Blacks' exclusion and denial of rights. Together, these stories, in the background, converge to provide context as well as weight to a tour making claims about Black Oklahomans as well as Black Americans' rights and belonging in the state and nation.

Black Towns, Black Communities

Besides North Tulsa, other areas known to have Black neighborhoods, Black "areas" (not necessarily spatially defined), or a sizeable Black population are incorporated into Black-town tourist efforts in a variety of ways. When the

Black Heritage Society tour that went to Oklahoma City entered the Oklahoma History Center and Museum, we were ushered into a large banquet room, where we were seated at round linen-covered tables bordering an auditorium-style stage. The event officially began when one of the museum administrators, a Black man, bounded up on the stage wearing a top hat and a tuxedo with tails and then began to tell us about the museum's investment in collecting, preserving, and displaying artifacts related to Blacks in the state. Speaking to the audience of bus tourists he said, "The way we can do this [collect artifacts] is through *your* contributions, family heirlooms, and *your* willingness to part with them. Museums are not like textbooks . . . they are not just words and images. [We] need three-dimensional [items]" (emphasis mine).

To illustrate the value of such work, he went on to tell a story about one of the museum's recent acquisitions: six hours of silent film, recovered from the attic of a recently deceased person, showing footage of Black Oklahomans in the 1920s. There was clear excitement in his voice about the find and what it meant for documenting Black Americans' contributions and roles in the state. "This is a rare treat," he told us. "You are the first group to see that footage." And with that the museum administrator proceeded to show the silent film, providing his own narration and commentary throughout the viewing.

THE FILM PROVIDED short takes of Black people involved in a variety of businesses: working in the offices of the *Oklahoma Eagle* and the *Black Dispatch*, Black-run newspapers in Tulsa and Oklahoma City respectively; people working in T. H. Elliott's Department Store in Muskogee, a medium-sized city in eastern Oklahoma; a woman getting her hair washed at the southwest headquarters of Madam C. J. Walker's hair salon in Muskogee; students playing sports at Tulsa's Booker T. Washington High School; girls at Muskogee's Manual Training School; people carrying a man on a stretcher at an undertaking business; and the graduation procession of Langston University, a historically Black university. Of all these takes, footage from businesses in the small city of Muskogee were shown most frequently. There were scenes from **Langston**—a Black town—but the overwhelming majority of the content depicted Black life in Black neighborhoods and establishments in Oklahoma's urban areas, leaving room for associating Black towns with a more extensive Oklahoman space than conventional definitions of the communities allow.

To me, the museum administrator seemed most interested in highlighting the film's significance as an indicator of Black Americans' importance and their connection to valuable resources from the past. So the images of life were as important to proving Black status as was the film technology itself. "That's a big thing," he said, rounding out the viewing. "If you knew someone to put you in moving pictures, you were home," he said, making the audience both familiar and Black by his reference to "you." A Black person had "made it," he went on, if the person knew someone with a motion picture camera. The film demonstrated Blacks' position and access to key cultural and material resources in the larger American society. With his constant use of "you" or "we," like Allen, he addressed the audience as if it were a community of like-minded/like-understanding/like-situated Blacks. "You" were home.

The visit to the museum included other activities. We were given time to take a self-guided tour of the Black Oklahoma exhibit, which showcased African American life and achievements across time. There was also a lengthy talk with an elderly and charismatic Black-town member, who told the origin story of the Black town he grew up in while also sharing recollections of his own life in the town. Most of the tourists were captivated more by the elderly man's words than they were by the film footage or the exhibit. They asked to pose for pictures with him and engaged him actively during the question-and-answer session. Besides the stop at Green Valley, hearing from this man was the only other "live" and interactive experience that we had with "official" Black towns and their representatives. That tourists were drawn in by the man's speech perhaps says much about how engaging he was as well as about tourists' interests in learning about town life. Yet from the perspective of the tour representatives and narrators, the film was the pièce de résistance. Its rarity and its ability to provide evidence of Black Americans as active in business and possessing valued material resources as early as the 1920s mattered much. In this way, although the tour exposed visitors to information about life in Black towns "proper," key tour narrators expressed the most excitement about indices of Black success that went beyond the officially recognized boundaries of Black towns.

Racism and Black Communities

It is not only bus tours that situate Black towns within broader Black communities and Black American identifiers. So too do other tourist efforts self-defined as Black-town initiatives at the larger state level. Indeed, my encounter with a state-sponsored group launching a Black-town project brought this home. I received a call from the mayor of Promise when I was sitting inside my apartment about twenty minutes away. "Karla? Some people from [the city] are coming over here, and they want to do something about Black towns. I know you're interested in the Black towns too. Do you want to come?" The mayor's voice sounded hurried, as if he were trying to get the information out quickly and encourage me to make haste. I jumped in my car and twenty minutes later arrived in Promise's town hall, where I found Mayor Marshall with three chatty and jovial women, two White and one Black. After brief introductions, we sat down at a table in the office and began to talk more about their purpose for coming to Promise. The woman who acted as the head of the operation, Lucille, explained that they began a project called African American Trails. Lucille also distinguished her agency's project from others in the Black-town tourism industry: "Our focus is African American experiences in Oklahoma with Black towns as the core." The goal, she said, was to have individual Black communities feature a storytelling event that reflected something signature about the place. They envisioned tourists, who would be provided with a trail map of sorts, doing self-guided drives to visit a cluster of Black towns, where they could stop to learn about the town by seeing a storytelling performance related somehow to town life. After this explanation, one of Lucille's colleagues added, "It isn't just Black towns. We want to use Okmulgee, Tulsa, Buffalo Soldiers. The focus is on African American experiences across the state." For the itinerary including Promise, they thought that tourists could travel a route encompassing Okmulgee, a midsize city, and Tulsa.

To assess whether Promise was a good site for the project, Lucille told Mayor Marshall, "We need to know what you think is a good story for Promise." Mayor Marshall was at the ready. He launched into a lengthy discussion of how the town got started and sustained itself. He also included many personal recollections of his own family experience and success, in both farming and small-business operations. He capped off his nearly ten-minute talk, laughing and saying, "You said you wanted a story, and I gave you ten!"

But it became clear that the women organizing African American Trails wanted something different. Lucille replied to Mayor Marshall, "We want to get an idea of things that happened. Did you have a problem with the Klan [in Promise]?" she probed. Mayor Marshall then offered a story that appeared to be exactly what the women were looking for. The story involved a light-complexioned Black man from Promise who had been voting in the county elections because he was presumed to be White. But once he took one of his darker-complexioned siblings with him to vote and was suddenly denied the right, he pursued a lawsuit that sparked a conflict and that made this story ripe for African American Trails. According to Mayor Marshall, the Klan showed up in Promise to hassle the man about his lawsuit, only to retreat when the men from the man's family and friend network came out on his porch poised with shotguns. The Klan, deterred by the strong and armed presence of so many Promise men, never returned again. Soon after, Mayor Marshall explained, the Suffrage Act was passed, and eventually Promise put up a commemorative sign recognizing the man who brought the lawsuit and stood up for Blacks' rights. There was quiet after the story, but the women were taking notes. This story, it seemed, was precisely the sort of thing they were looking for.

I followed the work of African American Trails for many months, was on their mailing list, and attended some of their planning meetings. At one meeting, occurring about a month after I met them in Promise, they discussed the work they had accomplished visiting various Black towns and communities and deciding which were good candidates for African American Trails. Promise was on the list. Indeed, when the discussion turned to Promise, someone at the meeting said, "When he [Mayor Marshall] came to the [part about the] men standing on the porches with shotguns against the Klan, it was a real story and reflected everything we wanted to do in this project." Other towns and communities that were on the list included a non-Black town for a storytelling event centered on its former Black hospital; a Black town with a story about early twentieth-century residents who joined in an ill-fated Back-to-Africa project and lost most of their property in the process; and a non-Black town's story about their Black school as well as, possibly, their relationship to a neighboring Black town. Thus, although the group stressed that the stories should be organic and meaningful to the towns and communities, particular stories seemed to especially grab and perhaps seem more marketable to the planners of African American Trails.

Racialized events and conflicts with race relations would be the highlighted themes. Black-town experiences were not about what typically has been regarded as making Black towns unique, such as their historic entrepreneurship. In African American Trails, Black towns and Black communities were linked by their experiences with racism, with iconic indices of America's pre–Civil Rights "race problem," such as encounters with the Klan and segregated institutions. When I asked directly about the project's intent, Lucille and her colleagues told me that the stories could be about anything that the towns wanted and felt defined themselves, whether contemporary or historic events. Lucille especially stressed that her background in community development prioritized letting communities decide their own path.

"It is up to the communities how they will market things," she told me. Yet it was also clear from the way the project unfolded and from the towns that were perceived as a good fit for African American Trails that certain identifiers of race, racism, and Black Americanness in the United States were the target. Although this was not stated outright, stories that highlighted Blacks' struggles with White racism, overcoming racism, and Black social success appeared to be of most interest. Mayor Marshall's family story and town business history, similar to the one Ben Walker told about Green Valley, was not a good fit. A run-in with the Klan was.

Over the next two years, the African American Trails project would hold two storytelling events, one in a non-Black town and one in a Black town. However, the plan for a self-guided tour of ever-available, site-specific African American stories did not materialize. Nor did the plan to work with all the communities originally identified. One-time events did occur. They included performed stories about the segregated hospital, about the ill-fated historic Back-to-Africa movement that some Black-town residents joined, and about the life of one buffalo soldier not specific to Black towns. Additionally, there was a traveling performance about the development of Black towns that included a broader focus on Black Americans in the state. But Promise's story never became a feature in African American Trails. A variety of logistics, including staff changes at the agency hosting African American Trails, probably impacted the momentum and reorientation of this project. Still, the attempt was never to single out a unique Black-town experience but rather to foreground Black towns within a larger focus on African American experiences, as the project organizers originally admitted. Reflective of the heritage-tourism genre, the focus was on events and figures deemed significant to a particular narrative of the Black American past. To fit within the story genre that suited African American Trails, large tropes of race in post–Civil Rights America were highlighted.

Honey Springs Battlefield

Honey Springs Battlefield, the site of Oklahoma's largest Civil War battle, became a feature of tourism in the state in the 1990s. The first-ever tour of the site was in 1963 for the battle's centennial, and this proved a catalyst for bolstering public attention on the historic event.[32] Through the National Park Service's American Battlefield Protection Program, the Oklahoma Historical Society (OHS) began acquiring acreage of the battlefield lands from private owners starting in the 1960s.[33] Over the next few decades the

Reenactment of Honey Springs Battle. Photo by author.

commemorative apparatus around the park was increasingly extended to include an interpretive center, trails, monuments, and additional acreage. In 1994 Honey Springs was designated a national historic site.[34]

Honey Springs is a common stop on bus tours of Black towns, especially those that tour eastern Oklahoma. The Black Heritage Society tours sometimes include Honey Springs, but specialized tours for visitors attending conferences as well as private tours have also been known to stop at Honey Springs. Indeed, this landmark, of which Oklahoma is quite proud, could be classified as a heritage site. It is on the National Register of Historic Places, and it is the site of a biannual battle reenactment. The reenactment takes place over a weekend and draws thousands of Civil War history enthusiasts. It is one of Oklahoma's biggest tourist events.

In 2008, I participated in a tour organized for participants at a conference. It was a voluntary tour for those who signed up, and our bus was about half filled with participants on that sunny weekday. Our narrator was a self-taught historian, Pat, who learned about Black-town history by reading voraciously about the communities. Less animated than Allen but seeking to keep the group engaged, Pat led us in a series of quizzes throughout the tour, often posing questions and asking for us to answer them based on the handouts we were given before the tour began.

Our first stop was Fort Gibson, the first military garrison built in Indian Territory and, on Black-town bus tours, often a precursor to a stop at Honey Springs. As we neared Fort Gibson, our tour guide asked, "What three American presidents lived at or near Fort Gibson?" There was silence and our narrator filled in the answer for us: "Sam Houston—president of Texas; Jefferson Davis—president of the Confederacy; and Zachary Taylor—U.S. president." She followed up with another question: "What year was [Fort Gibson] built?" A tourist knew the answer and called out, "1824." "Yes," our tour guide said, and added that the fort was occupied by the First Kansas Colored Infantry and later by two African American units that were brought into the army.

The existence of the First Kansas Colored Infantry, a regiment of Black soldiers recruited by the state of Kansas to fight for the Union,[35] is probably why many Black-heritage tours stop at Fort Gibson. The Kansas Colored, as they are commonly called, is the "Black part" of the fort (and of Honey Springs). Buried within travelok.com's description of the fort is mention of a Black presence at Fort Gibson, even though the fort is not situated in the African American History and Culture section of the website: "Fort Gibson also has a unique place in African-American history. From 1867 to 1873, Buffalo Soldiers served intermittently at Fort Gibson. Eventually, the outpost became the headquarters for the all-Black Tenth Calvary."[36] In our tour guide's narration, Black presence at the site was not discussed at length beyond a mention of the Kansas Colored's (or the Buffalo Soldier's or Tenth Calvary's) existence. The origins of their formation as a group, their experience as a regiment, or any race-specific experiences they had were not part of the narration, even though this information was available to us in the materials we were given. Indeed, once the bus stopped at Fort Gibson, the highlight event for us was a demonstration of how the oven in the garrison worked. While we ate deliciously warm bread from the oven, a man from the OHS, dressed in a Civil War military uniform, explained the ingredients and the techniques used for making the bread and gauging oven temperature.

We then boarded the bus again to head to Honey Springs. Among Civil War enthusiasts, the Honey Springs battle is one of the most significant and is often called the "Gettysburg of the West." As we left Fort Gibson, a historian from the OHS boarded our bus to tell us about the significance and events of the battle, which I jotted in my notes as he spoke:

The 1863 fight between Union and Confederate soldiers was over Fort Gibson and the Texas Road, along which resulted the battle site. Fort Gibson and the Texas Road were two areas that each side sought to advance control of what was then Indian Territory. Prior to 1863. Confederate authorities reigned over Indian Territories. Creek and Cherokee tribes signed a treaty with the South and then organized regiments. When, on July 18th, Union General Blount had his men march twenty-seven miles and nine hours south on the Texas Road, they fought skirmishes along the way and ended up at Honey Springs, where Blount's guns bombarded Confederate guns.

The OHS historian told the story effortlessly and in great detail, speaking as if he knew every element of the event. His account of the battle felt as if it were meant to captivate us with the intrigue of conflict, gore, and the battle's crescendo into the Union side's victory. In this way, the account was positioned as one of the tour's highlights.

The other highlight was a partial reenactment of the life of the Union soldier who fought in the battle. The OHS historian introduced his "associate," Rupert, an older man with a long, curly mustache and a deep Southern drawl. Rupert, who joined us on the bus, was dressed in a Union solder's uniform. He told us about the hard life of a soldier. I wrote, "In Oklahoma in July it gets hot and muggy. . . . It rained during the battle so soldiers' uniforms were wet. They were thirsty. And they would take coffee cups and fill [them] with water . . . [from streams] of Texas Road. Horses do business in the road so this is why more people died from dysentery." Giving us gritty detail like a historian, Rupert followed this depiction with an exercise, leading us off the bus and telling us to line up to participate in an army soldier's drill. Commanding us to face forward and, setting us up in perfect file formation alongside the bus, still in character, he shouted, "Now, everyone count off."

GROUP: Yes sir!
RUPERT: Now count off. One. Two.

Rupert had the ones step back. Then he dismissed one of us for not following orders and staying in line. Amid our stifled laughter, he had the rest of the group face forward and turn right, forming into a line. The action was complete when he explained, again leaving character, "This was the life of a soldier."

The stand-out facts of the battle and soldiers' lives are indeed the central aspects of narratives about Honey Springs. During the reenactment weekend, a series of tents house demonstrations of food and cooking, trade and craft skills, dress of the era, music, and more. The bus-tour visit to Honey Springs is no different: tourists are introduced to generic aspects of soldiers' lives during the time. A soldier's life in battle is the takeaway from a visit to Honey Springs, even when the visit is on a tour of Black towns.

In tourist brochures and historical accounts of Honey Springs, the battle is often described as representing a series of firsts or "onlys" among Civil War events. These mention that it was the largest battle in Civil War history that occurred in Indian Territory; the Union's win "opened the way for federal troops to control the Territory"; the battle involved a multiethnic group of soldiers made up of African Americans, American Indians, and Hispanics participating on both the Union and Confederate sides; it is the only Civil War battle in which Indians fought Indians; and it is a case where "Blacks [particularly the Kansas Colored Regiment] proved their qualities as fighting men," given the role they played in the battle's success.[37]

It is the last part—a piece related to African Americans—that likely provides the justification for including the battle site on tours of Black towns. Yet in the tours little is said about the Kansas Colored Regiment beyond the fact that it existed, participated, and was important to the battle's success. To be sure, the mini reenactment of a soldier's drill and the OHS historian's narration focused on the details of the battle and quotidian life for soldiers, without much attention to race, Black soldiers, or certainly Black towns. The broader tour highlights—the battle narration and the reenactment—do not cover anything specific or detailed about the Kansas Colored Regiment. Instead, the tour's key features are about the battle and the soldiers (as a general group), sources of historical information about the country's major moment, and also sources of entertainment for bus tourists.

What is more, even with brief mention of the Kansas Colored Regiment, there is no explicit attempt to connect the battle or the soldiers to *Black towns*. Why does a Black-town tour go to a Civil War battlefield, and why are Black-town tourists—who are there to learn about the history of Black towns— engaged in activities about how Civil War soldiers cooked bread and marched?

An irony of the invisibility of Black towns in Black-town tours of Honey Springs is that Honey Springs is a quarter mile from an officially recognized Black town. To get to the battle site you must enter the town of **Rentiesville**, one of the thirteen remaining Black towns. Yet the proximity of **Rentiesville** to the battle site is the exact opposite of how the two are inserted in

Black-town tours. They are seen as separate entities. The OHS historian mentioned that **Rentiesville** was founded partly by veterans of the Battle of Honey Springs, but he did not elaborate, and his next comment was to respond to a question about General Blount, about whom he is more of an expert. Similarly, Black-town tours visit Honey Springs and **Rentiesville** separately and do not relate the two. This is even though it is likely that some of the battlefield lands were and possibly still are owned by residents of **Rentiesville.**

Stretching out across three thousand acres, parcels of battlefield lands were acquired by the Oklahoma Historical Society starting in the 1980s.[38] There has been much written about how some property owners of battlefield lands were not and still are not willing to sell their lands to OHS, and the society has been careful not to appear to use force to obtain the lands. Given the closeness of the battlefield's official entrance—the portion owned by OHS—to homes on the road leading from **Rentiesville**, it is very likely that at least some of the homes of unwilling sellers are owned by **Rentiesville** residents. The contestation over land and belonging—the question of whether the land belongs to Honey Springs or **Rentiesville**—seems to play out in the tour where the spaces that count as Black history and those that count as American history are kept apart.

The battlefield is indeed part of a Black-town story—and the OHS historian acknowledged that, even if he gave the point scant attention. Yet the tours do not highlight that connection. Instead, when you go to **Rentiesville** as a tourist, you will learn about the background to two streets that form the intersection of the town: John Hope Franklin Street and DC Minner Way. You will hear information about the famous historian John Hope Franklin, and you will see where his house still stands. You will also visit DC Minner's blues club, a small club that is the center for an annual blues festival and for monthly jams. Before Minner died in 2007, you would meet him in the club and get to hear him play. Since his death, his wife will host your tour bus at the club. She will tell you about Minner's life growing up in **Rentiesville** and about how he left the town and returned in his adult years to start the club. If you were on the tour I took, you wouldn't have heard from her about Honey Springs, just up the road. For, in the tour, the appeal of Honey Springs appears to be its prominence in Oklahoma's contribution to American history. And the appeal of Rentiesville is its historic cultural richness led by Black Americans.

The Appeal of Black-Town Tourism/
Appealing to Black-Town Tourists

In Oklahoma's Black-towns tourism, the appeal of heritage (the significant past) has at least two distinct qualities: it is American and it is Black. It is American, located and tourable in defining American events, structures, and discourses. And it is Black, linked to specific peoples and places (that are or can be somehow Black-identified) but also connected to and read through American discourses of race that tourists can witness across a range of spaces, places, and sites. Sometimes blackness and Americanness intersect across different spaces. These intersections are made possible especially when the space of the tour is lifted out of Black-town remoteness, branching out to cities small and large, to major monuments and landmarks, to lands vast and remote across the state. But also, sometimes blackness and Americanness in the tour do not obviously connect and instead remain spatially and socially distinct. When they do not connect, Americanness is more likely to stand on its own, separate from blackness, than the other way around. In tour narration, the Civil War battle site stands out as a prominent feature of Oklahoman and American history with little known or shown about Black Americans or the relationship between the battle and Black towns. So, too, for the Oklahoma National Memorial. Even if tourists can discern or imagine connections between Black towns and these spaces, the tour narration does not do that work for them.

Yet when blackness and Americanness *are* connected, such as in the narratives by Allen or by the African American Trails project, Black-town heritage tourism normalizes Black towns by bringing the towns into broader spaces that possess clear markers of what America stands for and is. The tour shows the communities' and their residents'/founders' relationships and contribution to major and central processes while also claiming what is distinct and remarkable about them as Black communities that reached particular heights. Allen made an appeal about where blackness belongs and he made that argument in an appealing place. He made the case that the important history of a major American city is Black history. He built an argument that centered Blacks in the founding of the city and the state, and consequently about Blacks' rights in America. He built this argument for a receptive Black audience, arming them with information about not merely their history but also their centrality, worth, and rights in the nation.

The anthropologist Michel-Rolph Trouillot once lamented that Haiti is often viewed outside broad patterns of history and structure.[39] Because of its common identifiers as the first Black republic and the site of a major Black revolution, Haiti, he said, is treated as extraordinary and unusual. For him, the country should be understood as shaped within a set of patterns that engulf a wide swath of countries and places. Treating Haiti as an aberration, he cautioned, risks setting it apart and missing its relationship to and emergence from a set of organized structures and processes such as colonialism and slavery.

Black-town tourist events appear to work both sides of the coin that Trouillot references. The tours trade on Black towns' remarkableness: the Black-town triumph over odds, possessing the first Americans to found Oklahoma's second-largest city, the unusual place of Blacks in those processes and events. At the same time, tourist events are sometimes careful to place Black towns at the center of America's themes: racism, capitalism, the modern built environment, Civil War history, and so on. Reworking the space of the Black town is a key tool for this achievement.

To do the work of identifying a Black-identified place as both remarkable and normal, as typically American, typically Black, and yet unusually Black, is to do political and social work. Allen's work on the bus was political, which is not to say that it was inaccurate. African American Trails is also political. Trouillot thought there was a political agenda underlying efforts to mark Haiti as exceptional. Such efforts, he argued, bracketed Haiti off from normalcy. However, the political project that casts Black towns as normal and unique is somewhat different. The politics of the heritage tourism project enacted by Black Heritage Trails—steeped as it is in the racial politics of Oklahoma and the United States—is precisely to center Black towns in broader American contexts and discourses. It is sometimes to shift focus away from the idea of Black towns as ghost towns or relics of the past. In the hands of Allen, it is to explain and make a case for—to appeal to tourists about—how Black towns are deserving of their place in contemporary American narratives, just as Trouillot wanted us to acknowledge and analyze Haiti's place in the Caribbean and the world. The ways in which Black towns are accorded this place in American history and consciousness—or separated from it— vary across tourism events, to be sure. The narrative strategies employed by tour guides, town residents, would-be historians, and others are sometimes surprising and sometimes deemed problematic, sometimes highly effective and sometimes quite limited. But ultimately the towns themselves and the tourism that surrounds them both evoke and demonstrate the ongoing appeal of debates about whether and how Black people belong to and are an integral part of the American story.

CHAPTER THREE

Economic Futures

While Black towns are revered for their past, a common perception of present-day towns is that they are "ghost towns": denuded, depopulated, impoverished, and run down. If you look at Black towns on the surface or consult state and federal statistics, you might find these suspicions confirmed. Driving into any of the remaining Black towns in Oklahoma (those that are officially recognized as well as those that are unincorporated), you will see main roads that are barren. Cars pass along the roads fairly regularly, but there are not many. And those that you do see tend to be older sedans, some rusted and loud. The buildings lining what was once a main commercial thoroughfare often are in striking disrepair, sometimes abandoned and boarded up. Certainly, most buildings are not functioning as active businesses, and most (but not all) of those that are open serve a sparse clientele. Some city-center buildings clearly have experienced a fire. Many are surrounded by knee-high weeds. When you add to this the 2012 U.S. Census data revealing that across Black towns median annual household income is approximately $20,000, home values average $50,000, and each town's population is no more than about one thousand,[1] the picture of dire circumstances seems complete.

This perception of a devastated Black community fits into a larger and long-standing trope of disorganized Black places. However, a devastated small (Black) town also fits into a common perception of rural America as nonmodern, nonglobal, and anti-urban.[2] There are countless tales, scholarly accounts, and investigative reports of ravaged rural lives, of people living on the edge.

That said, for historic Black towns, is this image of an economically ravaged place complete? Black towns may have few or challenged physical and economic resources, but among their small populace there is much effort devoted to boosting the towns' economies and infrastructure. What's more, a variety of people are invested in Black towns and express hopes of refashioning them into vibrant, sustainable, and modern spaces. In the town of Wrightsville, you will find economic planning groups. In Promise, Wrightsville, and Newtown, you will see town council members rolling up their sleeves multiple times per year to write grant proposals for improving or developing infrastructure and businesses. All towns work with public utility

Pecan Street, main business district in **Boley**, Oklahoma. Photo by author.

companies to augment their facilities and services. Wrightsville and Freeland have tried to attract private investors to update town services and infrastructure. At town meetings in Black towns, people exchange ideas about
cleaning up community streets and buildings. Clubs and committees such
as "Make Wrightsville Beautiful" and the "Newtown Development Group" are
not uncommon. The narrative that rural Black towns are sites of poverty, no
longer living up to their past and holding no hope for the future, is therefore not a complete account of Black-town life. Black towns are indeed economically fragile, and many residents and outside observers talk openly
about that. Yet, the narrative of a "dead" Black town must contend with and
is sometimes muted by another narrative and by activities focused on modernizing Black towns to enhance their futures.

Black-town leaders play a large role in getting town improvement efforts
in motion. The mayor of Wrightsville was no exception. Along with town
council members, in 2008 he worked long hours to submit a grant to a federal agency. In 2009, the town received over $300,000 to work on reconstruct-
ing Wrightsville's downtown streets to make way for new businesses. After
residents had written so many grants without success and because few

Oklahoma towns won such an award, the funding represented a big coup for the city. With the downtown streets widened thanks to the grant, the mayor was eager to show me the community's plans for updating Wrightsville's commercial sector. He took me to meet the architect designing a vendors' market to be located in Wrightsville's city center. The architect was a young African American (but not a Black-town resident) and recent graduate of architecture school who had won awards for his work. Large and visually stunning, the design included numerous vendor stalls and a state-of-the-art-looking building for the overall structure. The idea was for the market to host vendors from Wrightsville and surrounds, including neighboring Carson—a predominantly White town—and even from nearby medium-sized cities that have a significant Black population but are not Black towns. The market would brand itself as a space on Black-town soil that incorporated and profiled producers and consumers regardless of their place of residence.

The vendors' market stands as an example of the various ways that Black towns exist in a state of becoming. The intense planning around the market and the excitement over its prospects reflect a desire to update the towns and make them more attractive to the contemporary American eye and interest. As Wrightsvillians were planning it, the market represented commercialism, up-to-date infrastructure, urban-rural interfaces, and even racial integration—reflective of American ideals and discourses in the early years of the twenty-first century. Emphasizing local crafts and foods to revitalize an economically challenged community, the market also tapped into some of the trendiest markers of desirable and contemporary lifestyles for urban and suburban America, notably locally sourced goods as staples for modern living.

Although residents and town leaders lament the passing of their economic and entrepreneurial heyday, there are many who simultaneously engage in efforts to rebuild the towns according to the terms of modern American society. Theirs is not a preservationist attitude bent on restoring what once was. Instead, efforts and imaginations for plotting town futures involve shaping, boosting, and expanding Black towns in ways that, in part, diverge from iconic indices of the Black-town past. There is still a priority placed on commerce and production—especially capitalist production and profit through small businesses. However, planners of futures for Black-town economies engage with the principles of a modern (sometimes neoliberal) economy as they think about how to move Black towns forward. They talk, for example, about the need for local, Black businesses but also about the value of attracting large industries or collaborating with other towns, regardless of the towns' racial identities. Nonresidents—"outsiders"—are also attracted to

Black towns, usually for the profit opportunity the towns offer them as potential property and business owners.

Identifying Black communities as in need of improvement and development is not new. The well-known 1960s report by Senator Daniel Moynihan,[3] known commonly as "The Moynihan Report," is perhaps the quintessential document leading efforts to identify and address social and economic problems in Black communities. Moynihan laid out Black communities as deficient due to their poverty, nontraditional (nonnuclear) family structures, and unemployment. Resulting were a number of public programs related to housing, jobs, and business development (to name a few) to "fix" Black communities. The outcome and reception of these efforts have been mixed. We know that Black residents in economically stressed areas have organized formally, informally, and successfully to uplift their communities.[4] Investments in this way have been high and extended, often to boost the image and profile of the community so that the quality of life improves, infrastructure is enhanced, public appeal is broadened, and pejorative images of the communities are questioned.[5]

Yet Black-community improvement projects—whether formal or informal—have also been fraught with tensions about the specific path that the projects should take or the implications of change being directed externally. As anthropologist Laurence Ralph has shown, state programs to build up Black communities have sometimes done more injury than improvement due to the kinds of limiting categories that the programs assign to Blacks.[6] So, too, for the trend in gentrification, which scholars argue has often led to the displacement of many Black (and Latinx) residents from their own communities.[7] Indeed, the picture of nonresidents or new arrivals improving Black (and Latinx) communities—whether as external agencies with programs for socially disadvantaged communities or as individual investors or new residents with a gentrification plan—is one of displacement, racial and class disparity, and partially fulfilled promises.[8] As such, while a range of people and groups have been drawn to Black towns to participate in remaking the communities, the outcome of the investment has been mixed, as is true of other Black communities in the country. Sometimes ideas to improve Black towns have galvanized the genuine enthusiasm of local residents interested in making their communities economically stronger. But at other times, economic and social improvement projects have disappointed those same residents, particularly when the projects have not been centered on local involvement, when they have been geared more toward profit accruing outside the towns, or when they have created social, racial, and economic disparity among town residents. One person's hope for profit is another's displacement and stalled hope for a better future. Black towns exhibit a dynamic that is most often associated with urban America but clearly also exists in rural areas.

Embattled, Yet Visionary, "Mom and Pops"

The backdrop to Black-town improvement planning is the current Black-town economic reality. As in much of rural America, where agriculture significantly slowed down in the mid-twentieth century, labor market opportunities have declined, especially since the 2000s, and employment rates are low compared to metropolitan areas.[9] Black-town formal economies are similar. Small businesses, once the hallmark of the towns' economic success, have been hard to sustain and no longer form part of the communities' economic profile. There are a variety of informal and occasional businesses, such as lawn-mowing services, Avon sales, or crafts retail, that people run out of their homes. These usually supplement residents' income from other sources such as employment in neighboring cities. Black towners of working age are much more likely to be employed somewhere outside the towns they live in so that they can make ends meet.

For those wanting to start a business, local establishments are also hard to get off the ground. If launched, businesses are challenging to sustain given the small size of the population and the need for garnering resources from "outside" to get the businesses going. Big corporate-led stores, particularly Walmart, offer rock-bottom prices and services in small-to-large cities within no more than forty miles of any given Black town (and usually closer than that). Accordingly, they are more attractive to income-stretched Black-town consumers. Walmart runs are a regular feature of everyday Black-town life. Despite the cost of the gas to make the drive, most Black-town residents do their regular shopping in large superstores anywhere from five to twenty miles away.

A comparison of Black-town businesses between the 1940s and the early 2000s shows the weakening of the communities' commercial base. The number of businesses from one town to another always differed. In the 1940s, when Black towns had double the population size that they do today, sociologist Mozell C. Hill showed that the town of **Boley**—the largest Black town—had more than sixty formal businesses, while the smaller town of **Rentiesville** had twelve.[10] In the twenty-first century, there are far fewer businesses across all Black towns as well as per town. Some towns now have

Closed Dollar Store, **Langston**, Oklahoma. Photo by author.

zero locally owned or locally run businesses or services, and the towns with the highest number of establishments do not have more than five. Of course, town populations have declined, but the proportion of formal businesses and services to the residential population has dropped off significantly. Compare **Boley's** high level of one store to approximately every fifteen residents in the mid-1940s to a maximum of two (usually fewer) formal businesses per every three hundred residents in the early 2000s.[11] As such, people who reside in Black towns can almost never obtain basic goods and services such as food and clothing, medical care, undertaking, or lodging in their community. Some establishments do appear — especially small food-retail stores — but their sustainability is often in question. Stories abound in Black towns about a local resident or aspiring entrepreneur from elsewhere who planned for or attempted to get a business going in a Black town, only to have the idea or effort thwarted.

That is what happened with the Wrightsville Convenient Mart on Poplar Street. I drove past the vacant store several times. You can't miss it. The store sits prominently off the busiest road dissecting the town, in a line of businesses that mostly appear abandoned. I admit that when I first saw the Convenience Mart's bright-yellow and new-appearing signage, I assumed it was a functioning establishment. That was until many people shared tales of how the store had recently and suddenly closed shop. Wrightsville folk were not surprised. They said they had warned the owner—an African American man who was not from the town—that keeping up the business would be a challenge given the ebb and flow of patronage and easy access to Walmart only twelve miles down the road.

After learning of this recent history and the status of the store, I drove past it. Unlike most days, I noticed three new-looking SUVs parked outside and the door ajar. Curious, I peeked inside and saw dining tables and chairs, and a cash register on the counter. There were a couple of glass-door refrigerators that are used to sell drinks, but there were barely any drinks inside; I saw only a couple of bottles of water. Inside the building, I saw three men (who, based on physical appearance, I presumed to be Black), milling about. One of them was visible behind a thin curtain; he was in a space that I later saw was a kitchen. I then saw a young person, likely in his twenties, walk in the store just after me and ask one of the men inside what they were serving and how late they would be open. "We have hot dogs and hamburgers." The younger man hurried out looking pleased. I sensed that he was planning to return to place an order, and so did the man in the store, who called out after the departing younger man, "You have thirty minutes before we close." With this encounter I sensed that, although the budding restaurant had only been around for a few days, word was already out about it.

What *was* the word? I approached one of the men who looked like he was working there and asked him to tell me what was going on in this store that had been closed just a couple of days prior. Casually dressed in jeans and T-shirt with a Bluetooth device in his ear, the man talked fast. He was brimming with excitement. He told me how he and his buddies—whom he referred to as "the seven CEOs"—were starting a restaurant that was going to practically "blow the roof off" Wrightsville. He boasted of their credentials: he had a culinary degree, and his partners had business acumen and experience in food service. They were going to turn Wrightsville around with their upscale, modern menu, which he handed to me while we were talking and just as he got a call and started speaking to the person in his ear. "I am busy talking to someone 'bout the business," he said. He removed the earpiece to focus on telling me more about the background and purpose of the seven CEOs.

None of them were local, he said. All hailed from a suburb of Oklahoma City, but he claimed they could get to Wrightsville (about sixty miles from where they lived) in forty-five minutes, so the trip would not be bad. "Why Wrightsville, then?" I asked him. He drew a personal connection: "I grew up in Piney View . . . and I was with an Upward Bound program that often took us on trips to Wrightsville in the seventies." For Black kids back then, he continued, "Wrightsville was like this," he said snapping his fingers low down by his side repeatedly and rapidly, to signal that Wrightsville was the happening place. So, he claimed, he wanted to bring all that energy back to Wrightsville, and his restaurant was going to meet the challenge.

His bragging nature and grandiose plans made even me skeptical, but there was no question that the man appeared committed and invested. He spoke mostly in superlatives about what the seven CEOs could achieve, and he exuded confidence about their plan. It was also clear that something was already happening inside that business, where there was a lot of activity and interest. So I put the store on my radar and made a point of checking on it when I was back in town. A day after discovering this Convenience Mart-turning-restaurant (which had no new visible name), I drove by and saw just one car parked in front of the shop and the doors closed. I did not see the fast-talking man, but someone passing by told me the place was closed so the owners could finish painting. A few days later I circled back and this time saw no cars and the doors still closed. Later I was visiting with a Wrightsville friend and mentioned that I noticed that the restaurant doors were closed, and my friend replied, "Oh, they closed that shop down. Something about they had a fire and won't be coming back." I heard no more about the business, why it closed, or what became of its owners. However, something made me suspicious about the idea of a fire, particularly since businesses closed and opened so often in Black towns, and I saw no evidence of a fire.

The closing of the revamped Convenience Mart left Wrightsville with one functioning business, a different convenience store that had been around for several years, run by Wrightsville resident Mrs. Hanson. A middle-aged woman who will tell you that she is "from Wrightsville," Mrs. Hanson spent the early years of her childhood in the town with her parents. Her father had been a prominent hotel owner in the community. Early in her youth she'd migrated with her family to several different cities in the West, before eventually settling with her husband in the metropolitan Oklahoma City area for more than thirty years. In the mid-1990s, she returned to Wrightsville for a visit, but on the drive back she said she had an epiphany: she should start a business in Wrightsville. Not just any business. A liquor store where she would also sell sundries. Now a widower, she began the process of returning to Wrightsville to execute her plan. Almost ten years later, her store is the only standing example of a late twentieth-century Wrightsville business that has endured. That it is run by Mrs. Hanson, a woman, also connotes the shifting landscape of Black-town economies. Compared to when her father was a lead entrepreneur in the town, as men were more apt to be, women now take a more prominent leadership role in Black-town economies.

Mrs. Hanson's store is run out of a modest building in need of repair; it sits on the main road across from the vacant Convenience Mart. It has a fair amount of traffic, which ranges from customers seeking to buy her goods to residents who congregate to socialize in the evening. The store became a literal "convenience" as well as a physical focal point. It was a place to pick up small items without having to drive out of town. It was also a social space, with residents congregating outside to chat and listen to music in the evenings.

Despite the relative success of the business, unlike so many other local businesses, Mrs. Hanson is the first to admit that, even with her relative success, running the store singlehandedly is not easy. She describes the labor-intensive process of stocking her business by making daily trips to Oklahoma City, an hour away:

> I spend three or four hours in Walmart shopping—tryin' to get everybody their, what they need, you know—what they told me they want—and, uh, I can only fill up—. I can usually fill up my basket three times—so I fill up my basket once, get in line, check out, take it to the car, come back, fill up my basket again, stand in line another thirty or forty minutes—whoo!—go to the car, take that, and then come back and get the rest o' my stuff. Then I have to go to the tobacco warehouse. Then I have to go to the liquor warehouse. Then I have to go to the, uh, there's two other warehouses I have to go to, to pick up supplies. And I'm thinking, this is, this is—. Every day I do this, and I'm so tired, and I'm thinking, this is crazy.

She comments often about her $4,000 credit card bill that she can't get ahead of. With the money and labor required, she wonders if the store is worth it, but her motivation is not the money. Her interest is in what the business does for her as someone whose self-esteem was at rock bottom after losing her spouse. She believes having a local business helps the community. "Most people that drink have some kind of concerns or problems. They're not drinking just for, to be social. So I get to witness . . . to the, uh, community that comes in the store, and give them advice on different things."

The larger personal void that the store fills motivates her to keep it going. So does her sense that she, a woman who has been involved in many town projects and has held leadership positions in town organizations, is providing a service for the town and thereby helping the community. Wrightsville appeals to her as a place that can be refashioned and revitalized. In fact, the store is only one of her ideas for how to boost Wrightsville. For although she is unequivocal that her store satisfies her own passion, she believes that "ma and pa businesses" are not what Wrightsville needs, since they will not survive. She thinks the town needs a major corporation that can provide jobs for town folks, and she is hoping to write a book about Wrightsville's history. In her mind, the book could be sold to generate funds for Wrightsville, linking tourism with the town's economic development.

Aspects of Mrs. Hanson's story are much like Celia's in Freeland, more than 100 miles from Wrightsville. In July 2008, I was on a bus tour that stopped by Celia's store, then an unassuming and barely detectable convenience mart or, as she called it, "corner store." It was housed in Freeland's inactive fire station. One of the tour narrators on the bus encouraged us to support Celia's local business by buying some of her cold drinks or snack items. The store was in an older cement building that stood just outside the center of town. Inside she had only a few items, such as chips, cookies, candy, and pop (or soda or soft drinks, depending on your brand of regional English) that you could see behind her as she stood at the counter taking orders.

Months later I would spend a lot of time in Freeland and particularly with Celia, a married mother of two in her forties who was born and raised in the town that she proudly called her home. She was an active force in the community, helping to organize festivities and working on community improvement projects. Her store was the only formal business in the town, and it was also a site where people congregated in the afternoons and evenings. By fall 2008 she had added stocked shelves that customers could peruse in the store's main room, rather than having to request items from behind the counter. There was a TV on constantly and tables that were usually occupied with customers or visitors. Every time I saw her she was boasting of developments or plans for her store. She was especially excited about it becoming a model for others to follow, whether in Freeland or other Black towns, so that Black towns could be more prominently "on the map." She showed me a second room off the back where she was going to add more tables. She also had increased her stock and was proud to say that customers were calling daily to ask her to get a specific item they wanted to buy from her.

To formally announce the store once business was taking off, she had a bright green sign made that read "Celia's Corner Store." Placed in front of the store, she hammered it in the ground herself so that people driving by on Freeland's main road would be sure to see it. But, like Mrs. Hanson, Celia was running the store on her own.[12] She had unpaid help from her daughter-in-law Darlene, a mostly stay-at-home mom with a toddler and infant and who was searching for ways to get out of the house. Darlene stayed in the store when Celia had to work at one of her other two jobs: doing clerical work for a local government office or working part-time as a cashier at a department store in Tulsa. After about 4:00 P.M. every weekday, Celia was in the store taking orders and selling her goods. And like Mrs. Hanson, she spent some of her weekday mornings, lunch breaks, or weekends buying goods to stock the store from Sam's Club or Walmart in Tulsa, about thirty miles away. There seemed strong interest in the store: customers were calling, stopping in, and hanging out. The place was never vacant, and Celia was always there working with a big smile on her face.

Yet by spring 2009 the store had slowed down, seemingly due to the burden it placed on Celia's time and, for Celia, due to the relatively slim customer demand. Because I had always seen people in the store and Celia was busy running from here to there to give customers what they wanted, I assumed that the store had ample clientele to sustain it. However, some people told me there wasn't as much support as Celia had hoped for. One Freeland resident who frequented the shop offered their theory for why that was. "It's the people 'down here,'" the person said, leaning their body downward while motioning their hand palm-down toward the floor. "The people who hang out in the town [center]. The ones that don't have barely enough to just survive every day. [They are] the ones that's big supporters." By contrast, this Freeland resident said, the more elite people in Freeland were "just comfortable" and so "don't think they have to support [the store]. They have what they need." This person called the phenomenon "jealousy" — others did not want to see Celia succeed.

The theory may be right. Certainly, the historical record on Black towns through the 1940s discusses degrees of class discord even if class hierarchies were not considered as marked as in communities where Blacks resided with Whites.[13] The person's description about what was going on with patronage of Celia's store spoke also to the fact that those who can afford to go outside the town to meet their basic needs do, even when presented with an option in town. Those with more economic and practical mobility to make and finance the drive to Tulsa (typically residents who were return migrants and had become more secure after living and working elsewhere) were probably going to the same stores that Celia did to stock her business, supplying their own homes with similar items. In Freeland, those without the financial and transportation means frequented Celia's store, perhaps out of need and lack of motivation. However, these were the same customers who could not afford to make large purchases from her. Her biggest clientele, those with less mobility and fewer resources, were those who couldn't buy enough from her to allow her to sustain the business.

Later, in 2009, Celia was denied a loan for expanding her store. Then the store began to take a drain on her time as she rushed from one job to another. Darlene's availability changed, and she could no longer open in Celia's absence. By May 2009 I noticed that the store was less frequently open. I would stop by during the usual post–4:00 P.M. hours and find no one around. I would call Celia or stop by her office, and she usually told me that she didn't have time to open the store and couldn't find someone who could open it for her. By June 2009 the store was closed. The sign still stood but the doors were locked and the former customers had migrated back to the front of the old school to hang out and socialize. Celia's interest in starting a local business that would not only enhance her income stream but also energize Freeland was challenged by constraints of time, material resources, and local support. Her business lasted longer than the Wrightsville Convenience Mart that was revamped by the seven CEOs, but Celia's interest in running a local shop would not reenergize Freeland's business base. In fact, the closing of her shop meant that Freeland was left with no local store.

It is noteworthy that two women, Celia and Mrs. Hanson, were both active entrepreneurs in their communities. If we think back to the iconic image of the town council men of **Boley**, who conveyed an image of Black respectability for Black towns one hundred years ago, we cannot discount the role of the women leaders in Black towns today. Indeed, not only are women like Celia and Mrs. Hanson active in Black-town economies; many Black-town women are also political leaders, and a photo of town council members today would likely be majority women. Mrs. Hanson and Celia may not appear to have high-level training in entrepreneurship or advanced business degrees, but it is striking that the two women with long-standing generational ties to the towns where they set up shop, rolled up their sleeves, and sustained businesses longer and more actively than the seven CEOs who were not "from" the community. That does not mean there are no men leading

Black-town businesses. At least two of the six formal businesses in the four communities I studied were run by local men during my research. Still, even as Black-town economies are precarious, women's significance in pushing things forward should not be overlooked.

Urban Inspirations, Suburban Aspirations

Simon Chester, a stout and impeccably dressed Black man, came to Wrightsville as an administrator tasked with serving as a liaison between an adult care facility housed in Wrightsville and the Wrightsville community. Part of his job included working with Wrightsville on the town's economic development to demonstrate the facility's commitment to the community. He came across as an energetic man with ambitious ideas and much excitement about mobilizing the town economy. "I'm really excited about [this]. Can't you tell?" he asked me when talking about his work with Wrightsville. In fact, in many ways, he possessed the vigor of the fast-talking man who proposed to transform the defunct Convenience Mart into a bustling, modern restaurant. If you were talking to him, he usually popped a bright smile and rattled off several ideas that he was convinced would transform Wrightsville into a vibrant place that, to me, seemed like a visual metaphor for the vibrancy in his voice. And he was talking to everybody—or trying to.

Unlike most employees at the facility, Chester lived in the town rather than in nearby suburban communities fifteen or more miles away, and he was often seen around town, walking the streets of Wrightsville and getting to know residents. He said he chose his residence purposefully, believing that if he were to work with the community on economic development, he had to be *in* the community. He said he was trying to connect with the community to get more of an "insider's" perspective and gain people's trust. And he didn't mean only people in prominent positions, but also those who were part of Wrightsville's everyday life.

> A lot of people would think that when you go in and you, you meet the mayor, you meet the chief of police . . . well you got it made. You know, I have a list of people. I got to meet Ms. Smith; I got to meet a lady named Ms. Holder; I've got to meet the blind lady that walks the street and has the most beautiful yard in Wrightsville; I got to meet the six or seven citizens that were at the city board meeting. I went around and introduced myself to every one of them. . . . I got their phone number, and I asked them where they live because I want to come visit

them. They all told me I could do that, so I'm going to go by, and I'm going to go by and knock on the door and just reintroduce myself, because that's how you garner trust with people.

He likened his approach to cultivating these relationships with the lessons he'd learned as a young Black man growing up and being raised by his mother and grandmother who taught him how to treat elders properly and with respect. When I asked him, he agreed that his approach was also to work from the grassroots, find out what the community wanted. If his ideas were not embraced by the community, well, he would develop new ideas. So, Chester's vision, as he described it to me, was to start with the community first, learn what the community wanted, and build from there. It reminded me of what the women leading African American Trails said about their community-driven vision for their project.

Chester formally launched his ideas for a community development plan at a June 2009 town meeting. It was a hot summer evening in the Wrightsville city hall meeting room, where the window air conditioner whirred noisily in the background but ineffectively cooled the space. There were more people than usual at the meeting—approximately twenty—perhaps in anticipation of Chester's proposal. Residents and company representatives sat in chairs asymmetrically assembled in the open space, facing the panel of council members who sat on the dais. Dressed in a suit and looking quite formal for the venue, Chester also appeared to be uncomfortably hot, as were the rest of us. Chester approached the front of the room and took a position at the podium typically used by special guests rather than residents. I had been up at that podium myself many months prior, introducing myself and my research. I recalled being nervous and was pretty sure that it showed. But Chester did not seem so. He proceeded to lay out a three-prong proposal of how to turn Wrightsville around. "What is Wrightsville community?" he asked as he stood before us in his neatly pressed suit. Answering his own question, he continued, "Wrightsville has cultural, educational, and historical experience." He likened Wrightsville to Zora Neale Hurston's Black-town homeplace of Eatonville, Florida, noting that Eatonville—with its reputation, popularity, and tourism—was a town that Wrightsville could learn from. To Chester, Wrightsville was a hidden gem that needed to be exposed. And how to make that happen? Chester proposed three ways: (1) pursue funding from the federal government, (2) create a "Miracle Mile" just like the one in Chicago, (3) update Wrightsville's housing. Starting with number two, "We won't have stores in Wrightsville," he explained, acknowledging the tall order for the small town, "but we want to establish a downtown area that we call Miracle Mile from Poplar Street to Baldwin Drive to City Hall." As he moved on to number three, he added that Wrightsville needed a new housing development to bring economic growth to the town. The increased housing would be possible if Wrightsville annexed with a neighboring area where new homes could be built. Chester then wrapped up:

> So, I'm asking three things: . . . To designate a Wrightsville Miracle Mile, a new downtown area that can increase property value, pride in the community, and growth. To establish an architectural review committee, because if Wrightsville wants to look like one of its *more popular suburban neighbors,* the town has to have certain types of buildings. And three, to put forth an ordinance to annex neighboring areas where new homes can be built. . . . If we grow the city of Wrightsville over the summer . . . we will see a whole new town [by fall] (emphasis mine).

Before this meeting, Chester told me that he envisioned Wrightsville as a bedroom community made possible by private investors. The community would be a kind of town where people who worked at the adult care facility would be able to live, but they could leave on weekends. With private investors developing housing subdivisions and businesses in the community, the town would have the accouterments necessary to attract bedroom community residents. It would be, as he told participants at the town meeting, like the "more popular suburban neighbors." And through what he called this "midterm solution," the town would benefit from taxes and other resources pumped into the community by the new residents. Thus, the "Miracle Mile" and annexation he proposed would lay the foundation for this plan to turn Wrightsville into an updated, quasi-suburban community with a downtown modeled after one of the most recognized American urban commercial districts.

Tag teaming with Chester at the meeting and providing the private-investor representation was Bob Jones, a White man and independent developer (not connected to the adult facility) who would build the housing development in the area that Chester proposed for annexation. Jones explained that he worked with his son and that he had purchased sixty-seven acres just west of Wrightsville that he had expanded over the years from eight lots. Their dilemma had always been that they could not get water for the site as they were turned down by both Wrightsville and the town on the other side of the property line, both claiming that the land was not within their city limits. Annexation would mean that Wrightsville would be able to provide them with water, the resource that, due to taxes, generates the most income for Wrightsville and most Black towns.

"We are not a political family or business," Jones insisted, seeming to reference indirectly the politics of his race for spearheading such a plan. "I'm aware of the political issues but I'm not getting involved in that. I just want to do a development. . . . I saw a need for housing in Wrightsville . . . an opportunity . . . I want to bring economic development [to Wrightsville] because I'm a businessman. [The housing development] will benefit the town because it benefits us. . . . I support development in Wrightsville. We will bring taxes to Wrightsville. The homes, at $125,000 to $165,000, will bring additional revenue for the city and lift the face of the city."

Jones wanted to signal that the plan was "purely economic." He admitted it was for his own financial benefit. Still, it was also for Wrightsville, as a community in need of expansion and revenue. Together, Chester and he stressed the richness of Wrightsville—not necessarily its racial history—and their interest in accentuating or "developing" that richness for the community's economic gain. This was not a plan to bring in affordable housing or businesses to meet local housing needs. It was a plan for upscale, rural living by bringing in people able to pay for higher-end lifestyles on which they could be taxed. Turning blighted areas into attractive, infrastructurally upgraded spaces would draw in wealthier outsiders who would "stimulate" the economy. This was not Mrs. Hanson's economic development plan, where her store served the existing residents at a level they could afford. It was a "trickle down" model of modernizing Wrightsville. Jones and Chester wanted to make the town more alluring to outsiders whose presence and investments in housing purchases and potential business creation would filter into the town's economy (and also into Jones's coffers) and broader profile.

Note, too, that the plan for modernizing Wrightsville was led by two nonresidents whose proposals called for introducing new residents and consumers into the town. Wrightsville had long received input and even initiative from administrators at the adult care facility when it came to economic planning for the town, to promote community-corporate relations. The formal setup stemmed from the charge of the liaison office tasked with guiding some form of community development for the town. But in this instance parts of the plan were out of the ordinary. For one thing, the plan included a nonemployee of the facility (Bob Jones) who made his case before Wrightsville residents, emphasizing how his strategy was meant to promote the economic advancement of the town. Jones focused on the business investment for his son and himself and the tax revenue that would generate from it *for Wrightsville*. Moreover, in Chester's case, even as he advocated for a Miracle Mile à la Chicago's shopping strip, his plan called for developing the buildings and improving the streets to make way for new establishments rather than building up local businesses or drawing on local talents. As he said, the goal was not to develop existing stores in Wrightsville but rather to make the town more attractive to tourists and to outside businesses that might set up in the town. Outsider intervention for community development and modernizing were critical to the plan.

This economic development plan for Wrightsville's future resonates with contemporary forms of gentrification and urban development. Indeed, Chester referenced success models in major American cities and suburbs that Wrightsville could draw on to improve the town. However, Jones and Chester put a rural twist on urban gentrification. In fact, while urban gentrification of Black communities is more widely known to us, rural gentrification is precisely what Jones in particular was describing. In rural areas of the United States and the United Kingdom, scholars have documented transformations in rural nonmetropolitan markets in which there is a rise in the number of large homes owned by people who have relocated to take advantage of lower property values. These people may be retiring or seeking to establish a second, "getaway" home in an idyllic, "counterurban" countryside.[14] Rural gentrification is associated with a higher level of living for new arrivals in depressed rural communities, creating the kinds of social chasms that have marked urban gentrifying neighborhoods.[15] Studies stress that class differences emerge with rural gentrification,[16] but that is because most cases of rural gentrification have been documented in predominantly White areas. It appears that no one has explored what happens in predominantly Black rural communities, however. Some hints about what might happen can be seen in the reactions to Chester's and Jones's proposals.

The Wrightsville leadership, which placed Chester and Jones on the meeting agenda, supported the proposal. But, without much surprise, some Wrightsvillians attending the meeting raised questions and offered comments: "How will the grant money benefit Wrightsville?" "How will Wrightsville be able to accommodate the proposed area to be annexed given the existing water problem in the town?" "Miracle Mile should be routed so that it doesn't miss existing businesses that can benefit from the expansion." "Wrightsville needs improvement in other areas such as with trash removal and road repairs." "Wrightsville needs to focus on restoring its historic monuments and buildings."

In the active discussion that ensued, there were questions—in some cases a degree of skepticism—about whether and how the plan could be executed. There were also clearly questions about how existing residents would fare in the process. Would the community's current needs and resources be sidelined or neglected? By implication, residents were asking: Will there be a qualitative gap between the new and the old? Will bringing in new resources mean the neglect of what is already there? Townspeople also made suggestions for amending or refocusing the plan, going further than Chester recommended. Some recommended expanding development of the community beyond the proposed plan. To these questions and suggestions, Chester (who responded most often) stressed that, with his three-point plan, Wrightsville would be much improved, economically and infrastructurally. The town would possibly gain more recognition and interest from potential taxpaying residents and from investors.

The plan moved forward fairly quickly. All three parts of Chester's proposal were approved at the meeting. A vote at a subsequent meeting to approve annexation also carried forward. The boundaries of Wrightsville's borders were expanded to incorporate Jones's proposed housing development. The streets bordering the Convenience Mart and Mrs. Hanson's shop were widened and improved to mark and make way for Miracle Mile. However, Jones's housing development was slow in getting off the ground, and an existing but inactive three-store retail area that Chester sought to revamp and revitalize remained fairly sleepy. On the other hand, the vendors' market (the design for which the mayor was excited to show me) developed as an outgrowth of Chester's plan after it was approved. It became a major economic development project that signaled an interest, among the town leadership and some residents, in the contemporary approach to modernizing Wrightsville as an inclusive and updated space with broad national appeal.

White "Investments" in Black Towns

Although Bob Jones's efforts did not get off of the ground as much as other parts of Chester's proposal did, Jones's remarks and interest signal an increase in White investors' attraction to Black towns. This is the reason that some residents consider the communities to no longer be "Black" towns. In the early twentieth-century model of Black-town economic success, the flip side of supporting Black-run and -patronized businesses was disengaging with Whites. At least according to the research of my grandfather, Mozell Hill, Black towners believed in maintaining distance from Whites who were thought to hold Blacks in oppressive relationships and to prevent Blacks from thriving as a group and in their group endeavors. He coined the term "White avoidance" to capture this phenomenon that he observed.[17] Hill said that Whites were always part of Black-town life as patrons of Black businesses, occasional employees, politicians in search of Black-town support, and, although taboo, romantic interests of Blacks who were resident in the towns. However, he also stressed that class and generation divided residents in how willing they were to engage with Whites. Elite and younger residents were more open to interacting with Whites, especially in economic and political life, while older, founding, and less wealthy residents advocated distance from Whites at all costs. Hill contended that, regardless of differing opinions, there was an overarching principle about "avoiding" Whites, and all residents were familiar with the principle, which was generally upheld. Residents regaled him with stories of their efforts to run Whites out of town when they attempted to work or start businesses in the community. There were also detailed accounts of Black towners who became alienated from the community after they attempted to work with Whites, and also of Whites who were pushed out of the community if they tried to set up businesses: "Last year we ran [out] two White men from the vicinity trying to open stores. One man didn't want to leave because he had a nice grocery store but he was dynamited. A White man own the cotton gin now, he bought it from a Negro. He tried to live here during the harvest season and we ran him out. We're not going to let the White man take what our parents work so hard to get. I'd rather die."[18]

Today, excluding Whites from business and economic life is not the Black-town plan. People openly recount their unequal encounters with White individuals or White-led institutions in Oklahoma. Yet, speaking to me, most said they believed that having Whites in their community is acceptable, if not, for some, preferable. Investing in and attracting large corporate employers of Black-town labor (as Mrs. Hanson supported) or engaging in local commerce and investments that are not racially defined or targeted *is* part of a Black-town plan. Imagining what today's Black towns can be means thinking about collaborating with neighboring predominantly and historically White towns (as with the vendors' market) as well as drawing in and on the skills and products of White service and business professionals. It means inviting a range of people, goods, and amenities to participate in building up Black towns. It means broadening the space of what constitutes a Black town.

Yet although Whites are welcome, and residents generally say that they do not care what race a resident or potential resident is, it would be wrong to assume that Black towners think race does not matter. Remembrances of the racialized and racist past are central to how residents think about why they want to build their towns up. That the towns stood up for themselves in an intensely racist nineteenth- and twentieth-century America motivates people to ensure that the communities go forward. If they are engaged in dialogue, Black towners are frank and critical about some of their current individual interactions with Whites that they know are marked by power imbalances and stereotyping. They sometimes express misgivings and hesitations about Whites at the same time that they make remarks about positive experiences with Whites or express strong convictions that Whites can and should be incorporated into Black-town life.

Rob Blue, a Wrightsville man in his late forties, told me that it wasn't until he was required to go to an integrated school that he had any social interaction with Whites. Even though there was a White town just two miles away, it took him going to Carson High School (after the Wrightsville school closed) for what he called his racial "separation" from Whites to change. By the time I met him, however, he had a different perspective about how the town should interact with Whites. "I think people that come here want to be positive for Wrightsville," he told me. "I don't care what color they are. . . . I got a White friend right now I can call and say, 'Man I need . . .' and he's coming." In many ways, there is clarity among Black-town residents that America is not the oft-touted "postracial society," but at the same time, they think racial inclusion should be a goal. Rob Blue thought it should be. The more organized planning for Black-town futures, by Black-town residents and leaders, centrally includes that goal. At the same time, the ways that some Whites are drawn to Black towns and engage with the communities reflect the realities of a postracial society not yet achieved.

Today, Whites play a much larger role in Black towns than they did a half century ago, and whether setting up businesses or purchasing property in Black towns, they are part of the contemporary Black-town economy. In fact, as you can see in the Wrightsville plan for a vendors' market and the proposal put forward by Bob Jones, Whites hold a place in efforts to "develop" the Black-town economy. Sometimes that place is alongside Blacks as producers or consumers of goods for sale in Black-town spaces. Other times, that place is as owners, developers, and even appropriators of Black-town businesses or property from which White owners turn a profit. In many ways, these efforts represent trends at the intersection of rural gentrification and counterurbanization—they involve private developers and other nonresident individuals who propose to acquire and transform local property for beautification or "development" as well as for their own profit-making or professional benefit.[19] Even though Black towns are rural spaces, economic development trends (especially those involving Whites as newcomers and investors in Black towns) mirror the displacement effects and racial/class divides occurring with gentrification in urban communities. Whites may be drawn to Black towns to acquire land on which to settle or profit, and some Black residents may even support this trend. Yet the social division patterns linked to urban gentrification resonate with what we see in twenty-first-century Black towns.

To situate Whites as investors in and gentrifiers of Black-town economies, it will help to understand where Whites are positioned more generally in Black towns. Recall that most towns' residents identify as Black or African American.[20] In Wrightsville and Newtown, by my count, between one and three Whites reside in the town center either as members of family households made up entirely of White residents or as domestic spouses or partners of Blacks who are resident in the towns. These individuals—either as home owners, renters, or nonpaying occasional domestic partners of Black residents—circulate in the towns and are known to other residents. In the case of family households and some domestic partners, they have lived in Black towns for lengthy periods, upward of five years but sometimes over twenty years. In Freeland and Promise, Whites are not present in central districts but they reside within town limits. These include a handful of new arrivals, a couple of whom are permanent residential partners of Black residents.

The remote White presence in Black towns first came into view for me when I took a ride with Mr. Bains in his older Ford pickup truck to see the full scope of Freeland. "It might smell like fish," he warned me about the truck. He said he would have been fishing if he weren't driving me around, which he had offered to do when he met me at the Freeland Town Council meeting a few days before. I said I didn't mind, and I actually never noticed a fish smell. The sound of the truck's motor and the creaks the body made on the dirt roads we ambled down were more of a nuisance. I kept having to ask him to repeat himself. By this point I had already been around Freeland, so I felt as though I knew the landscape in the town center. Celia and others at her shop had helped orient me. So I was paying more attention to Bains's information as we left Freeland's main square and headed out on a long dirt road that looked fairly uninhabited. "This is King's Prairie," he told me. We passed a couple of trailer homes, but mostly the road went through open space. He said it used to be farmland. "Farm up over here on this side. Over there" — he pointed — "they had pasture and hay." But no one is farming there anymore. And there was no post office. There used to be an elementary school, and for secondary school students went to Freeland. However, at some point King's Prairie was annexed to a small city east of it. There are no longer any schools in King's Prairie.

I asked Mr. Bains if King's Prairie is a Black community, and he said yes, but then he pointed out homes along the way that he said were inhabited by Whites. Later, we entered Jewel, another satellite Black town to Freeland, and I heard myself say "whoa" as we approached a very large brick home set far back from the road with an imposing gate. After seeing the more modest homes and vacant lands along the drive, and familiar with smaller homes in the town center as well, this house seemed to pop out of the clearing. "A White family lives there," Bains said. I asked him more about the family, and he didn't know all the answers. He said they had moved there from California, but whether they had Oklahoma roots he didn't know. It seemed unlikely he would know so little about someone in the center of town. People meet up at the town square, council meetings, and senior lunches. They bump into one another at the post office. So they often know the comings and goings of one another, the job or health status of members of their families, and more. But about this White family outside of Freeland's center, and gated off in their home at that, Bains knew little.

Based on my conversation with Black-town residents, it appears that Whites began settling on the periphery of Black towns (but still within Black-town borders) sometime in the 1970s. This pattern seems to have accelerated in the 1990s. In part motivated by land prices but also by land-sale advertisements placed by Black-town leaders, Whites began purchasing lands in the towns' outskirts and forming a kind of "White-ish belt" around town centers that remained predominantly Black. In some cases, Whites have been settling in areas that lie within the zip code of a particular Black town. Yet, as with King's Prairie, those areas represent named, unincorporated settlements bordering town centers. Thus, Whites in these areas are officially *in* the community, but they are unofficially outside, living on the perimeter of the town proper based on the naming process and informal boundaries drawn in the community. The area that Chester and Jones

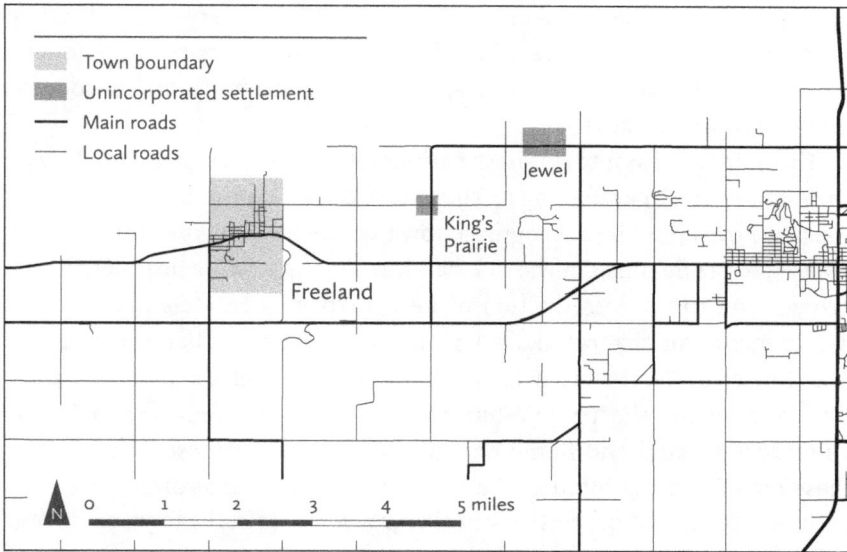

Freeland and adjacent Black communities.

proposed for annexation represents an example of the outskirts of a Black town that is made up predominantly of White residents.

This pattern is not that of the "Black belt" often described in Chicago, where Blacks were congregated in a corridor in Chicago's South Side and excluded from White neighborhoods that formed in the east and west regions of the city.[21] The inverse occurs in Black towns. Whites live in a residential ring around a Black-town center. In that ring, they often exhibit higher levels of income than existed in the impoverished and marginal Black belt of Chicago. In a sense, there is residential segregation between Blacks and Whites as there was in Chicago's pattern, but Whites are mixed in with some Black homes in the Black-town periphery. Blacks seem increasingly sparse in that space, and those that are there have been there for a long time, whereas Whites are more recent and growing in number. Additionally, the quality of life is different between the "White-ish belt" and the city center. The Black-town core is economically diverse, with low-income residents (mostly Black, but some White and American Indian) who, residentially, are mixed with middle- and upper-middle-class residents. The more economically elite are usually return migrant retirees who improved their socioeconomic status by living and working outside Black towns during their peak working years. Upon their return they build large homes, which are interspersed with public-housing homes, creating a very diverse housing landscape in the town center. The ring or belt around many Black towns, by contrast, includes some Blacks, but Whites are more highly concentrated in those outskirts.

The number of Whites in these peripheral town areas still does not reach the number of Blacks making up the larger towns—periphery or core—but the move by Whites into recognized town spaces has not gone unnoticed by Black-town residents. On the one hand, residents express openness to the growth and to the introduction of new, taxpaying residents. They even sometimes argue that racial diversity is a good thing for their town, just as Rob Blue said. On the other hand, they express regret about the apparent difference in how the newer White residents are living compared to Blacks. Difference in land and home beautification is sometimes at the core of these regrets. People compare the manicured lawns in parts of the periphery with the abandoned properties and overgrown weeds in the town core. People also notice the size of the newcomers' homes. That race is the subtext of these distinctions is not lost on Black residents, some of whom struggle to reconcile their belief that racial diversity is a contemporary social good with an observation that racial disparity is not, all within the same example.

Some residents of Wrightsville expressed that type of tension when they talked about their observation of Whites moving into Black towns, especially in response to how homes and land owned by Whites appeared. I sometimes heard Black residents simultaneously lament how White homes looked more impressive than Black homes due to the homes' size, quality, or aesthetics. Yet, those same residents could simultaneously sound pleased that, in terms of appearance, these remarkable White-owned homes and lands were raising the profile of their community. One person we interviewed called it a "beautiful sight" to see manicured lawns, and that same person felt that the ways in which some White properties in Black towns looked could be an example for Black residents to follow. However, this wasn't an argument that Blacks in Black towns were negligent in how they kept their properties and that the differences between the appearance of Black and White homes was due to a cultural difference or, worse, a cultural deficiency on the part of Blacks. Rather, an argument I heard from some people was that they wished Blacks could achieve homes that appeared as impressive as White ones. They wished that there wasn't racial disparity when it came to property beautification and ownership. They welcomed the high social value of aesthetically pleasing properties owned by Whites, while they wished Whites weren't dominating at this, especially in a Black town.

To me, people expressing this view wanted to be okay with Whites moving in, to be current in attitudes about racial diversity and race relations. But they also couldn't help but lament that what relatively recent White residents were modeling in Wrightsville created a chasm and an appearance of racial inequality on Black-town soil. They might have wanted Blacks to mirror how Whites were maintaining property. But they also did not like that Whites were getting ahead of Blacks, buying and excelling at maintaining land especially in a Black town. It seemed they wanted to be up-to-date and accept a racially diversifying town. Yet the inequality associated with how that diversification unfolded did not sit well with some. Their views also revealed their sense that Whites and Blacks living side by side doesn't indicate racial harmony, even if they indicate that their racial diversity is a "a societal ideal."

In addition to Whites settling peripherally in Black towns, there are also Whites who are acquiring property and investing more remotely in Black towns in other ways. From everything I was told and saw, there is nothing harmonious about this development. Unlike Whites who purchase and take up residence on Black-town lands, there are Whites who become absentee property owners. They reside in neighboring non-Black towns and purchase Black-town property that has been foreclosed when Black-town owners have defaulted on their property tax payments. In Wrightsville and Promise, people told me about Whites who watch tax records to see whose property will go up for cheap sale due to delinquent payments. Once they take ownership of the defaulted property, they hold on to the land rights without using the land. Then they attempt to resell the land to the original owners on a payment plan—at a high interest rate, allowing the White buyer to turn a tremendous profit. White land buyers—some Black towners call them "investors"—trade in Black-town lands as though they were participating in a predatory payday lending scheme; payments are made in installments that by some estimates are five times what the White buyer himself paid for the land. The practice, therefore, represents a different kind of "White investment in Black towns" than the gentrification model discussed earlier. Unlike Bob Jones, who also sought to turn a profit through the purchase and resale of Black-town property, the land buyers acquire land that cash-strapped Black owners are forced to abandon; the White buyers' "investment" in Black-town property is based on the resale terms they set. Unlike Whites settling on the periphery with an interest in putting down roots, these "White investors" are only interested in the resale potential of Black-town lands. They do not appear at Black-town meetings to make a plea for support, as Bob Jones did. They do not reside in the community, even in the physical periphery. Because they are not physically present, they are remote, although their impact is upfront and real.

Promise is a town where this type of "White investment" is active and legendary given the extensive "investments" of one particular land buyer, John Turner. Turner lives in the county seat about twenty miles from Promise, but his name is widely known in the town. That is because he owns a majority of the land in Promise, and residents have witnessed his land acquisitions and resale over a long period. They also know stories—some of them personal stories—about Promise residents who were in debt to Turner as they tried to regain their property from him by getting into a long-term payment arrangement.

County tax records show that in 2012 Turner owned a number of lots in Promise. His name appears on more than two hundred land deeds in the county where Promise resides. Not all of the property Turner owns is listed as within the town of Promise, but, by my estimates, at least one-quarter of it is. Raymond Ray, a Promise resident who has looked at the county records himself, estimated that a handful of nonresidents like Turner own approximately 80 percent of Promise's thirty-four hundred lots, and that Promise residents own the other approximate 20 percent. Ray recounted a story of one of these nonresident White buyers—perhaps Turner—who tried to make a deal with him:

> This one fellow, he had bought this land. He paid less than a thousand dollars for it. It was a house—. There was two houses on the land. And he sold one of the houses. And I had a house down in Pineway [a pseudonym for another Black town], which I had bought for my mother back in the sixties, and this one fellow, he wanted the land. . . . So this same fellow that's investing in all this property at these tax sales, he told me, said, "Ray," he said, "I have six lots up there at Promise. I will trade you straight up for the one that's two and a half you own in Pineway." So, I did. . . . So that's the property that the fellow sold—traded—me, and so I remodeled the house and use it as a rent house right now. Uh, but he only paid . . . paid less than a thousand dollars for it. But the land that I traded him down there in Pineway . . . he sold that to a [Pineway] fellow for five thousand.

This is the word around Promise about Turner. He reaps a steep profit either by trading the land to people like Raymond Ray who want to acquire property in the town, or by reselling to original property owners at a much higher rate than he paid. Raymond Ray pointed out that he, too, was trying to make some money from land purchases and sales. In fact, he estimates that he owns a sizeable portion of Promise land himself, and thus nonresident Whites like Turner are not the only ones participating in land buying and trading in the area. But the land-trade deal that Raymond described resulted in a large profit for the nonresident White investor. Based on Raymond's story, Raymond benefited because he got rid of land that he wanted to sell, but the "investor" made out better in the transaction because he sold Raymond's land for more than five times what he paid.

Gina Simms told of her family's dealings with Turner when I asked her if she considers Promise to be a Black town. She implied that she does not believe it to be when she replied that there are Whites in the town. She used Turner as her example and described him as a "White man buying all kinds of places around here," but she gave an emphatic "No!" when I asked if he lives there. However, for her, his presence was enough not to classify Promise as a Black town. "He [only] wants the land to sell to you," she explained. We sat in the living room of her small, modest home as she recounted the story of how her family was impacted by Turner's "investments." Her sister told Gina that she forgot to pay her property taxes, so she lost the land to the county. Turner bought the land when the county put it up for sale. "I said to my sister, ask Turner will he sell it back to you," Gina said. The sister did, and Turner told her she would have to pay him five thousand dollars. "I think he might have paid a hundred and something dollars when he bought the land," she continued before explaining that her brother was stuck in a similar bind. Turner bought her brother's land after he didn't keep up with his tax payments. "My brother . . . said [to Turner that] he didn't have that money, and Turner said [he can] pay [it] back monthly [at] $100 a month. He will be paid [off] at the end of the month. [He] almost has it all paid off. He done paid him $5,000."

Turner's position in Promise points up an aspect of the spatial economy of racial inequality and diversity in Black towns. Whites are clearly present in Black towns, as they always were.[22] But in many cases they are spatially and economically separate from Blacks. Whites are especially visible on the outskirts of many towns as resident property owners, or they are less visibly in the town—but still very present—as absentee owners of lands in the town center. Blacks who are centrally located in the town but also economically fragile may lose their land to an absentee White landowner. Or they may not have the resources to build up their property to the extent that Whites do on the town peripheries.

Both groups of Whites — resident owners and absentee land owners — are drawn to Black towns by economic incentives: cheap land to purchase or to turn a profit on. These dynamics that position Blacks and Whites unequally are not enough to lead Black residents to speak of "White avoidance" as Hill observed seven decades ago. To the contrary, some Black towners invite White involvement in Black towns, and others, like Gina Simms, do not consider their communities to be "Black towns" due to the presence — physical or remote — of White property owners. Black residents sometimes struggle with the White presence and the inequality associated with it, but they stop short of saying that Whites should not be allowed to reside or invest in Black towns.

The Unfulfilled Promise of Prisons as Development

The state of Oklahoma is another external investor in Black towns. Besides the state-run adult care facility in Wrightsville and public facilities and services such as senior lunches and health clinics, the state maintains its presence through correctional facilities in two towns. In the 1980s prisons entered the towns of **Boley** and **Taft** after a state campaign to augment Oklahoma's corrections apparatus focused especially on rural areas. The claim was that more prisons would address overcrowding in the state's two existing prisons while also bringing jobs to blighted rural areas. **Taft** and **Boley** were a draw for state prison development, then, because they were poor rural communities where prisons were touted as a means to turn the local economy around, especially by providing employment. Bob Jones claimed that his housing development would pump revenue into Wrightsville; state representatives claimed prisons would do the same for **Taft** and **Boley**.

But prisons serve the neoliberal economic and political designs of the state and of private capital rather than investing extensively in the communities where they are sited.[23] They also are built ostensibly to safeguard the security of the nation, usually from Black citizens, who are disproportionately represented among the incarcerated population.[24] Thus, despite how prisons were advertised to residents, prisons in Black towns — like prisons elsewhere — have not been designed to meet communities' economic needs. Given the disproportionate number of incarcerated Blacks in the United States, prisons' placement in predominately Black spaces might seem a tragic irony. Moreover, there is little evidence to support the idea that prisons can serve as a mode of economic development for small towns.[25] Sociologist John Eason is one of the few who argues they can.[26] He found that for a small prison town in a rural Black community in Arkansas, prisons were a help. Residents were happy about the chance to have their town's image remade by the introduction of a major industry.

Eason's findings may not be applicable to all small, rural Black communities.[27] The dashed development plans described by most researchers of prison towns would be disappointing for any community. Yet, for a *historic* Black town like the ones in Oklahoma, they are especially problematic when the community was founded on a principle of integrating institutions with the social needs of the community for the enhancement of a racially marginal and threatened population. Besides the array of businesses that Black towns boasted into the mid-twentieth century, the largest Black towns offered locally run institutions and services for youth and adults with "special needs" or for social skill development or rehabilitation. These included reform and training schools for Black youth as well as facilities for adults and youth with mental illness or physical disabilities. Some of these institutions were turned over to the state around the 1950s and no longer strictly served Black residents, although they were major employers in Black towns. Even as state institutions, at that time the facilities remained very local: they were integrated into Black-town daily life as institutions for Blacks. According to the stories I heard from residents, Black youth at the facilities socialized in town with resident Black children. Black parents who came to visit their children living at the facilities interacted with Black-town residents, who sometimes offered their homes for parents to spend the night. Black-parent visitors also frequented Black-town businesses. Thus, for sixty to seventy years, the care and development needs of Black youth and adults were met through Black-town infrastructure that eventually became coordinated with a state apparatus.

Prisons in Black towns represented a shift in this setup. The state's first prison, Oklahoma State Penitentiary, was built in 1908 (a year after Oklahoma became a state), and one year later the Oklahoma State Reformatory was added to the state corrections apparatus. These two prisons served as Oklahoma's only prisons for more than six decades, until the 1970s, when Oklahoma introduced a plan to increase the number of prisons. As did many states across the United States at that time, Oklahoma's Department of Corrections cited prison overcrowding as the reason for the expansion.[28] Most of the state's prisons built after the 1970s ended up in small towns, and all were state run until 1995, when private prisons were introduced.[29] By the early 1990s fifteen of Oklahoma's state prisons were located in rural areas or small towns, mirroring a national trend of siting prisons in nonmetropolitan areas.[30]

Between 1983 and 1989—the early and end period of state prison construction in Oklahoma—three of fifteen nonmetropolitan prisons in Oklahoma were placed in Black towns. However, unlike most rural prison siting in the United States, none of the three prisons were newly constructed. Rather, buildings that once housed Black-town institutions were transformed into correctional facilities, leaving the structures that were originally developed to serve Blacks' social needs standing, but changing their purpose and constituents. Jess Dunn Correctional Center, which opened in 1980 in **Taft** as a medium-security prison for men, replaced **Taft's** mental health facility for Blacks, which was constructed in 1932 and later became a juvenile home for Black girls and boys operated by the Oklahoma Department of Human Services. John H. Lilley Correctional Center opened in **Boley** in 1983 as a minimum-security men's prison. The building was originally constructed in 1923 as a tuberculosis sanitarium for Blacks. In 1925 it became a training school for Black boys, and in 1965 it was turned into a facility known as the **Boley** State School for Incorrigible Negro Boys. Finally, Dr. Eddie Warrior Correctional Center, a minimum-security women's prison, opened in 1989 in **Taft**. The prison building previously served as the Haloche Indian mission school, built in 1906. The mission school later became the state-operated Industrial Institute for the Deaf, Blind, and Orphans of the Colored Race in 1909 (commonly known as the DB&O), which endured until 1961. Between 1961 and 1989 the building housed a center for Oklahoma children with a range of special needs. In all cases, the prisons were named after the Black American directors of the facilities when the institutions served Black towns and Black people in the state.

These physical and symbolic connections between the state and preexisting Black-town institutions did not reflect the nature of the qualitative relationship between state prisons and town life. Consider economics. The institutions that preceded prisons in **Taft** and **Boley** employed up to 25 percent of the town population,[31] at a time when local work opportunities had become scarce with the retreat of local, privately owned businesses. Yet in terms of local employment,[32] by the time I began my research in 2004 (thirty years after prisons came to **Taft** and **Boley**), residents in both communities could count fewer than five town residents (less than 1 percent of the town population) who worked at the local prisons. Thus, it appears that prisons did not boost employment as residents hoped they would.

Almost anticipating this outcome, residents of both **Taft** and **Boley** protested the arrival of correction facilities in their towns. They opposed prisons on their soil not for concern about their safety—concerns that often

State prisons in Oklahoma's Black towns

	Jess Dunn Correctional Center	John H. Lilley Correctional Center	Eddie Warrior Correctional Center
Location	**Taft**	**Boley**	**Taft**
Year Built	1980	1983	1989
Gender of Inmates	Male	Male	Female
Level of Security	Medium	Minimum	Minimum
Prior Institutions (Year of Opening)	Mental health facility for Blacks (1932); state juvenile home for Black boys and girls	Tuberculosis sanitarium for Blacks (1923); training school for Black boys (1925); state reform school for boys (1965)	Indian mission school (1906); Industrial Institute for the Deaf, Blind, and Orphans of the Colored Race (DB&O; 1909); Oaklahoma Children's Center (1961)

Sources: Gray 1988–89; Hill 1946b; O'Dell n.d., "Taft"; Oklahoma Department of Corrections 2002; Stuckey 2009.

motivate opposition to new prisons. In fact, **Boley** residents claimed that dealing with boys from the reform school was challenging enough that they could not imagine the community would be any less safe with incarcerated men in their town.[33] Instead, residents in the two communities feared losing the jobs provided by the existing institutions in **Taft** and **Boley**. Along with others who argued that Black towns were sited for prisons due to racial inequality,[34] these residents worried especially that prisons would not fulfill local labor needs, presenting a *new* gap between the community and the institution.

In addition to leaving an employment and economic void, prisons represent a socio-spatial gap between the community and the institution as, despite their obvious existence, prisons remain remote from town life. On the one hand, in both **Boley** and **Taft**, the prisons have a commanding presence. Due to their large size in small towns, they are hard to miss. To visit **Boley**, your only option is Route 62, and you cannot avoid seeing the sign for John H. Lilley prison just off the side of the road. You'll see the sign before you turn down Pecan Street, **Boley's** main road, where all the town's businesses and former businesses are located. You also cannot miss the prison itself, up on a slight hill, a large and expansive brick complex. Similarly, coming in to **Taft**, you can see Jess Dunn prison from the town's main artery, while Eddie Warrior prison sits a few hundred yards from about a dozen homes in one of the town's most active residential hubs. When people give directions to a place in the middle of **Taft**, they use Eddie Warrior as a reference point; out on Route 64, they use Jess Dunn.

Yet physically present and spatially centered prisons are set apart from the town in other ways. The walling off of the buildings is both symbolic and physical. As in all prison towns, the prison structures in **Boley** and **Taft** are separated from the towns by large wire fences and gates. The fences that surround the buildings at Jess Dunn and John H. Lilley prisons are visible from the road and are a reminder of the prison-town barrier. Even Eddie Warrior's metal see-through fence, which allows townspeople who live and drive close to the facility to see prisoners walking about in daily activities, sets a clear boundary: few residents have ever gone beyond the fence walls or know much of what goes on inside. When prisoners move beyond those fences to perform work assignments in the community, they carry the boundary with them in the form of an "inmate" label on their prison garb.

Prisoners indeed move about the towns doing clean-up or construction work, and they have even sometimes marched in local town parades. Still, these are occasional and relatively brief moments. Everyday interaction in **Boley** or **Taft** has little connection to what goes on inside any of the three prisons or to the people who are resident inside them. People in both towns know which town residents work at the prison, and each town government has a relationship with the prison warden for logistical purposes regarding taxes or security. However, the regular routines inside the prison and inside the town rarely intersect and certainly not to the degree that occurred when the buildings were social institutions for Blacks.

The separation of prisons from town life was also shown in the content and distribution of the documentary *Sweethearts of the Prison Rodeo*.[35] The film tells the story of Oklahoma's prison rodeos, in which incarcerated men and women train and compete for the annual state sporting event. **Taft's** Eddie Warrior prison is the women's prison that is profiled in the film, which focuses on individual women competitors, their stories of incarceration, and what the rodeo means to them. Although the film gives the viewer context for the prison and flashes that it is located in **Taft**, Oklahoma, when it captions the prison name, nowhere in the film is the town of **Taft** described or explained. The film tells nothing of **Taft**, Oklahoma, as a Black town or of the history of the prison facility and its relationship to the town. Rather, the

Jess Dunn Correctional Center in **Taft**, Oklahoma. Photo by author.

story is focused on everything inside the prison gates and the spectacle of the rodeo.[36] Just as those gates are a barrier between the town and the prison, so does the film portray not only a separation but a nonexistent relationship.

I was aware of the film and waited for it with anticipation, expecting to glean some useful information for my research. In the summer of 2009, when the film was first screened in Oklahoma and the announcement was made that it would be shown first at Eddie Warrior, I expected that it would be a town event. However, when I bumped into someone from **Taft** and mentioned that the film was going to be showing that week, the person—who was well-connected in the town—was not only unaware of the screening; he was unaware of the film's existence. I viewed a few talkback sessions with the filmmakers after the documentary screened on HBO and noted that, in telling their story of making the film, they never mentioned **Taft**. Even with the prison an arm's reach from residential areas in **Taft**, they had evaded the town entirely.

In many ways, this gap between prisons and prison towns is not surprising or unique. Prisons' inaccessibility may seem hardly worthy of mention, since their purpose is to remove people from society. However, for Black towns built historically on hosting institutions that serve the local population so that the community is a source of support for Black residents, the introduction of prisons is emblematic of the multiple ways that Black towns have seen a monumental shift in the role and nature of local institutions. For some of the elder Black-town residents, prisons' placement in this shift has been a sore point, given the very institutions that prisons in **Boley** and **Taft** took over.

Ethel, a resident of **Taft**, demonstrated the idea of a socio-spatial chasm between prison life and Black-town life during an interview with me in 2008. Ethel was in her seventies at the time of the interview, and she lived alone in the town's public housing. I often saw her at the senior citizen free lunch provided by the state, and one day I asked her if I could interview her about her life in **Taft**. Like some other residents whom I talked to, she spoke of today's **Taft** as being "dead." But when she mentioned this absence of "life," she quickly followed by mentioning the Deaf, Blind, and Orphan Institute (DB&O), the facility for disabled and socially marginal Black youth that existed for fifty years in **Taft**. Ethel, like other **Taft** residents I met, mentioned the DB&O as an example of **Taft's** active and energetic days. One person described the DB&O era to me as "the good old days." Ethel said that when she was younger she was "at the DB&O" all the time, playing with children she befriended there. Her cousin even married a woman who had been a resident at the DB&O, and Ethel referenced their relationship as an example of the connections that developed between "DB&O kids" and "**Taft** kids." Although she drew a distinction between the two types of children with these labels, she repeatedly spoke of regular bonds between the two.

School was her biggest example of the DB&O/**Taft** relationship, because she considered **Taft** schools and the DB&O as "one school." "When they mixed the schools (the DB&O and **Taft** schools) it was beautiful," she said. Her reasoning was about the enrichment experience that the relationship provided for both. Reminding me of Mrs. Jessup's praise of her school days in Wrightsville, she said, "You meet all different people, get exposed to different ideas." By "mixed," she meant that DB&O children attended the town schools rather than having separate instruction inside the facility. That "mixing," she said, opened up new worlds. She also demonstrated how "**Taft** kids" accommodated the "DB&O kids" when, proud of herself for remembering, she broke into sign language. She learned to sign in **Taft** schools because anyone attending the school, she said, had to learn the language so that instruction was accessible to all enrolled students.

However, Ethel lamented that the days of DB&O/**Taft** integration are gone. "That was a long time ago that **Taft** and DB&O kids went to school together. . . . Once they quit that, **Taft** became dead," she said, sounding disappointed and again using a term that announced **Taft's** demise. The DB&O closed in the early 1960s, and **Taft** schools closed in the 1970s. The DB&O was replaced with another state home for children, the Oaklahoma Children's Center, which was not for children of any particular race. Although Ethel did not say whether children at that institution attended **Taft** schools, the school closed a decade afterward, and so, certainly, any interaction between the center and **Taft** schools would have been shorter-lived than what existed between the DB&O and the town schools.

When Ethel was sorry about the DB&O closing and being turned into a prison, I was reminded of Priscilla Dunlap's despair over the loss of Cromwell School in Promise. Losing the school means losing the town. Recall, too, Mayor Shelton's caution about school loss: "You lose your being." But, the fact that the DB&O eventually turned into a prison represents another layer to the story of school loss. The building had long ceased to be a school by the time it became a prison, and the town did not experience the loss of the DB&O simultaneous with Black youth being funneled to inhospitable White schools. However, the social meaning that town residents like Ethel attached to the DB&O faded even more. Ethel was unnerved that people inside the prison "can't get out," and while she didn't draw a clearer connection, it is hard to separate her concern—as a Black woman in a Black town—from the deep association of twenty-first-century U.S. prisons with the high levels of incarceration of Black males.

Indeed, Ethel's point was larger than the schooling relationship. She was talking about the kind of integration between town life and town institutions that existed prior to the 1960s and the qualitative shift in the organization of life in **Taft**, including the arrival of state prisons. As did many other residents in Black towns, Ethel felt a shift in the degree of connectedness associated with the town and the DB&O. As she also talked of the loss of stores and social activities that had helped **Taft** stay vibrant, for her, the end of the DB&O days coincided with a broader shift in which other town institutions and businesses were on the decline or, as she put it, "dead."

Ethel moved on to talk about **Taft's** prisons as emblematic of a qualitative shift in the town. Indeed, she equated the post-DB&O days with a different way of life: a disconnection between institutions, activities, and people in the town that contributed to the sense of the place being "dead." And, with this, she expressed concern for people inside the prisons, who she felt were symptomatic of this qualitatively different place. "Prisoners can't go out and move around as with the DB&O," she said. "People can't roam around. They can't get out. The community is different with prison," she said, characterizing the difference in freedom between DB&O kids and prisoners. It was as if she was likening prisoners to DB&O children, both in an institution and both deserving humane treatment. The DB&O kids could move about the town and enrich **Taft** residents' lives by interacting with people and getting to know them. Prisoners, by contrast, were locked up inside and couldn't get out. They were stifled, as was the town with the separation of town and institution.

Thus, Ethel points to the socio-spatial gap between prisons and the community that, for her, is a wholesale transformation of life in the community. The gap is one of a social and physical distancing between the institution and the town. The gap is brought, in part, by the spatial immobility of prisoners who cannot exchange with townsfolk and enrich them. But there is also a social distancing between the residents inside the institution on the community's soil and the residents who live in the town. The lack of relationship among people who are in the same town was what she saw as new and different, if not regrettable. Moreover, for her, there is a spatial contradiction. On the one hand, the institution is spatially centered in the town, and because of this prisons are known well by people in the community. At the same time, prisons and prisoners are largely unknown. Prisoners may be out on work release in the community, but their daily life is a mystery. They are on work detail overseen by prison staff and must stay focused on their task before returning to the prison. They do not enrich town life with a social exchange that prior town institutions for Blacks were set up to do.

The Appeal of Fragile Economies and Economic Futures

In the late nineteenth to early twentieth century, an appeal of Black towns was the economic futures they could spawn, raising also the social profile of Black Americans. An appeal of Black towns today is, ironically, their fragile economies. That is, many people and institutions are drawn to Black towns to transform their economic condition or take advantage of it. However, it is important to recognize the differences among actors drawn to Black towns' economic potential: Mrs. Hanson returned to start a business as her father before her had done successfully. Simon Chester promoted a community economic development model to urbanize Wrightsville. Turner grabbed land from poor residents. The state promoted prisons as a way to boost town economies. The picture is mixed. On the one hand the energies that go into the towns' economic development projects are high, revealing a strong vision and hope for Black-town futures. In that vision, fragile Black-town economies can be remade, if not restored. For people like Mrs. Hanson, Celia, and even Simon Chester—who worked and resided in Black towns—the appeal of Black towns is driven by a personal and professional investment in the community. They want to improve the quality of life for residents as well as improve the towns' public image. The appeal is also what Black towns can become—Black-town futures.

On the other hand, some energies are driven by what Black-town economies are. There is an appeal held by the towns' poverty and by what investments can yield. Indeed, some individual and state-level interests in Black-town economies are tied up with motivations for profit and social control. These energies, drawn especially from people located outside Black towns, are also high but emerge from a different place. John Turner and the state of Oklahoma approach Black-town economies from a distance. They siphon resources, including residents' money and property, or the town's physical landscape for purposes that serve nonlocal interests. The "benefits" of their "investments" flow out of the towns. As such, they engender social chasms and divisions in Black towns, which many residents regret or struggle with. Those divisions are marked by racial and class inequities and power differentials that play out in the configuration of everyday uses of space and lived social experience. The overall picture is that prospects and efforts for engaging with Black-town economies engender different sorts of struggles for Black-town residents, due to the challenges of either developing and maintaining locally sustainable businesses or living with the impact of non-locally organized economic ventures within Black-town borders.

CHAPTER FOUR

Community of Blackness

You don't have to be a White "investor" or gentrifier to be interested in going to a Black town as more than a bus tourist to learn about Black-town history. You also don't have to have a profit motive. In fact, Black people go to Black towns, some regularly and some for special events. Maybe they used to live in a Black town and routinely visit to see family. Some Black-town churches draw in Black Oklahomans living elsewhere in the state, and Black-church pastors often are not locally based but instead commute to the towns to lead services. Black people living outside the state also come to Black towns, especially to attend reunions, festivals, and rodeos. There are even those Black newcomers who opt to move to a Black town for the first time, with scant—or no—prior ties to the communities. So Black movement into Black towns is different than it was when the communities first started. People aren't fleeing the strictures of legalized segregation. They aren't called by Black activists to come help build an all-Black space. Even with the messages about a successful Black-town past but not present, there are a number of people who are motivated, encouraged, or excited to come to the communities today.

Who are these twenty-first-century migrants and visitors to Black towns? In her book *Call to Home*, anthropologist Carol Stack introduced us to Black adults who, searching for work in the pre–Civil Rights era, migrated from the Southeast to the Northeast. And then, in the late twentieth century, they returned to their home place, Burdys' Bend, in rural North Carolina.[1] What led them to go back to the place of their youth is not like what led them to depart the South. They wanted to reconnect with the place of their childhood, a place where they had family and other social ties. What brings them back "home" is similar to the stories of so many who move (back) to Oklahoma's Black towns, permanently or temporarily. Not all who make that move have roots or experiences in Black towns like those described in Stack's book; some are arriving for the first time but still looking at the community— often as a *Black* community—as some aspect of home and connection.

The Brookings Institution reports that the trend of Blacks moving from the North to the South, as Stack documents, began in the late twentieth century.[2] While some comprising this "New Great Migration" are professionals and retiree-transplants making a first trek southward, others are return migrants.[3] In Oklahoma's Black towns, the transplant is indeed less common than the returnee and the visitor. But all three types—transplant, returnee, and visitor/spectator—come to Black towns, and, in migration theory parlance, these people are more pulled than pushed. It is true that there are complex reasons behind their arrival in a Black town, but what resonates in their stories, and what I observed in their activities, is the pull of a Black space—the chance to be part of, (re)connect with, and perform within Black community.

In 2009, folks in Newtown organized and launched a new initiative to revitalize the town. The group's title, Newtown Will Rise Again, hinted that the plan was to "bring back" Newtown to its historic place of prominence. About thirty people showed up at the first meeting, exceeding anything I had witnessed at monthly town council meetings, which in all the Black towns I studied almost never included more than twenty attendees. At this meeting, made up not only of Newtownians but of interested parties from across the state, there was clear excitement in the air. Many of us walked in carrying the flyers that we had picked up or been handed somewhere in recent weeks, as if these were entrance tickets (though no such ticket was required). Seated at three long conference-style tables in Newtown's Community Center, we faced a master of ceremonies perched on a stage before us. Before the meeting got started, he had us introduce ourselves one by one. Among us were people of varying connections to the town. There were current residents, of course. But there were also town leaders; present and former employees of town businesses who did not reside in the town; former residents; Black professionals from Oklahoma's major cities; and even a prominent Black leader in the state. And, of course, an academic researcher. Word had spread widely that Newtown was organizing, and the advertising suggesting that something important was about to happen led people to want to engage.

A Black man and woman seated together introduced themselves as a couple that had just moved to Newtown. They had arrived from Arkansas and, two weeks before, had moved into a home they had purchased, near the center of town. The woman excused their appearance, mentioning how tired they still were from the move and unpacking. As she finished up explaining her excitement about being part of Newtown, there was a round of applause that I sensed was both to welcome them and also to acknowledge delight that someone would choose to move into a rural Black town.

Indeed, by this point, I knew that such a phenomenon occurred rarely. Black people who did not grow up in a Black town did not tend to pick up and move into the communities. I could count on one hand the number of people I met who fit that description. There is indeed an incredible amount of migration that circulates around Black towns. Yet new Black arrivals from elsewhere are not a significant part of that movement. More numerous are those people who moved out during their adult and preretirement years, the many return retirees looking to settle back in the town of their youth (a town they always called home no matter where their movement led them). There are also those who come back to take care of elderly parents. Also common are those who move in and out of Black towns on a temporary basis: as tourists, festival attendees, workers, and friends of residents. The White person who purchases a large-ish tract of land and builds a home on the outskirts is also, as we saw in the last chapter, a clear and known Black-town "type," even if relatively few in number. So too is the White person who moves in due to a partnership with a Black-town resident. However, the Black person who relocates to a Black town without having a history of permanent residence in the town is not consistent enough to be classified as a pattern or type.

And yet, although as new arrivals the couple moving to Newtown is an anomaly in Black towns, they are not alone. Across Wrightsville, Promise, and Freeland, I encountered four other Black individuals who, like this couple, willingly moved to a Black town as adults for the first time. There are likely others whom I did not meet. Among those I met, their primary reasons varied. One family was motivated by distant family connections and land access, another came because of an interest in farming and being more agriculturally self-sufficient, and yet another moved to a Black town for the chance to spread a message of racial unity. These are the reasons they mentioned first when asked what led them to move to one of the towns. However, in talking further with them it became clear that the Black identity of the place and the chance to forge ties with Black community was a significant motivator.

Why talk about these anomalies? Their stories counter those of the typical Black-town resident who has longer roots in the town, even if those roots have been unevenly planted, disrupted by a Black towner's movement back and forth during the peak adult migration years. The stories of Black-town transplants — as well as occasional visitors — allow us to consider what leads someone to purposefully seek out a place like Promise, with no grocery store or convenience mart, or Wrightsville, with its water crisis and abandoned buildings, or Newtown after it just closed its last school and the town leadership has expressed concern about the community's future. Looking at those who come to attend events in a tiny town with a bunch of boarded up buildings allows us to consider what their participation in town events means for the community, a Black community, as well as what draws them to a small Black place.

The people I met and observed who purposefully came to a Black town—sometimes for the first time in their lives—were searching for the chance to connect with their Black family. They were searching for the chance to engage with Black people to help "the race." Or, they were interested in just being part of a Black social space. The people I observed coming to attend Black-town events were actively engaging in what social scientists call "sociality," which is another way to talk about community, relationships among a group of people connected by locality or identity. The people who engage in that community may not share all things in common or even agree on the value or meaning of what connects them. In fact, complete accord due to shared identity or location is not likely, and negotiations of difference are necessary. Still, the Black people I observed coming from elsewhere to Black towns relate with the space or with other Blacks in the space in ways that prompt dynamic, ever-evolving relationships or reflections on those relationships.[4] The relationships and interactions—Black sociality for Black newcomers or visitors in Black towns—occur at the intersection of the town (a place, a community) and a Black identity, two features that draw Black people to Black towns.

Little Leaguers and Lowriders in the **Boley** Rodeo Parade

Booker T. Washington may have helped brand **Boley** as the early twentieth century's entrepreneurial crown jewel of Oklahoma's Black towns, but, arguably, the **Boley** Rodeo (and its accompanying parade) has helped make the town a popular destination today. As I talked to Black towners from across the state and asked them which other Black towns they had visited, **Boley** was at the top of the list. If anyone had been to another Black town, **Boley** was usually the one and the annual rodeo was the reason. Along with **Rentiesville's** Dusk 'til Dawn Blues Festival,[5] which occurs every Labor Day weekend, the rodeo is one of two top Black-town festivals, in terms of the numbers it draws, its scale, and its notoriety. These are the major Black-town tourist events that supersede Black-town bus tours with respect to the number of annual participants. It is estimated that twenty thousand people attend the rodeo in a given year,[6] and because it is such an important event for the community, the **Boley** Chamber of Commerce starts planning for the next year's rodeo the day after the last one ends. By far, the rodeo is also the biggest activity that the town relies on for revenue, particularly once **Boley's** successful, locally owned meat-curing business, Smokaroma, closed in the early 2000s after more than forty years in operation. But while the economic importance of the rodeo cannot be understated, the social significance is also an undeniable boon for the community and its Black-town identity.

The rodeo goes back to **Boley's** founding years, specifically to 1905, when the town organized a carnival and used the event as a recruitment tool to entice more people to move to the community. The carnival was a celebration for Juneteenth, the unofficial holiday among people of African descent marking June 19, 1865, when enslaved people in Texas were informed of their freedom. Historian Melissa Stuckey describes **Boley's** 1905 event as a "Juneteenth like no other." The week of June 22 was devoted to a slate of featured speakers (including one on behalf of Booker T. Washington), a parade, rides, games, and rodeo events. Advertising for the carnival was extensive and helped bring five thousand people to the town streets over the week.[7] According to Stuckey, there was high energy and excitement among organizers and attendees:

> Hungry crowds packed the local eateries like the Morning Star Restaurant and the Jones and Trimble Café. They also thronged the food stalls that lined the streets to purchase barbecue, watermelon, lemonade, candy and other treats. . . . Each day people and vehicles, from rickety ox carts to fine carriages, crowded the streets. They came to see the town, meet its people and observe for themselves the freedom and opportunity it might offer them. . . . They admired the homes, churches and the public school that anchored the community. They marveled at the miles of surrounding farmland, owned almost entirely by Black people.[8]

According to Stuckey, the 1905 **Boley** Carnival was a "celebration of Black freedom and a preview to attendees of the quality of freedom they too could enjoy in **Boley**."[9] This is both because the event was attached to Juneteenth (June 19) and because the life of the town was on display. The intended audience was Black people, and Blacks especially benefitted from the event by witnessing and participating in Black achievement.

Boley is still promoted in what is now the **Boley** Rodeo and Bar-B-Q. The two-day festival, which takes place over Memorial Day weekend, includes a street parade on Saturday afternoon and two evening rodeos, with details of the event and the town presented in a thick rodeo souvenir program. Older

Boley Rodeo and Bar-B-Q Festival souvenir program.

programs from the 1970s and 1980s detailed the different rodeo activities, such as calfing and bulldogging, to orient the spectator to what they would see in the rodeo arena. More recent programs provide less of this. Up to thirty pages in length and put together by a town committee, the glossy booklets contain a statement about **Boley's** history, photos of town leaders, and ads, which make up more than 70 percent of the content. Businesses in neighboring towns such as Okemah and Paden have been taking out ads in the program for more than three decades, publicly congratulating **Boley** on another rodeo event and helping to endorse the annual extravaganza. Former town residents also post ads informing about their families' ties to and love of the town. The program, then, is much about pride in and endorsement of **Boley**.

Additionally, the Oklahoma Department of Recreation and Tourism's website, travelok.com, lists the rodeo under its "African American Events" section. Because the event is featured on a state tourism site in this way, the target audience isn't necessarily Black people and certainly it is not uniquely Black. Nor has the souvenir program been pitched explicitly to a Black audience, since recent editions of the program have extolled the community's benefits as a peaceful place worthy of retirement. No particular retiree group is specified. However, through travelok.com's packaging of the rodeo as an African American event and the program's highlights about **Boley's** history as a haven and engaged entrepreneurial space for Black people, the rodeo is identified as being a Black activity.

Today's festival signature events are the parade and rodeo. Although the rodeo is the feature, the parade to me seems a larger social event. The daytime hours of the parade are more conducive to families as well as to people making a day trip from other parts of Oklahoma, since the rodeo begins at 8:00 P.M. and goes past eleven. Moreover, because people start arriving hours before the parade begins, and the street is a bustle of activity in anticipation of the event, the entirety of the parade experience may take up more time than the rodeo activities. The procession itself is relatively short (under an hour), but people line up early and wait for events to begin. **Boley's** main artery, Pecan Street, becomes an active social space, filling with spectators starting late in the morning. By early afternoon, Highway 62, which runs perpendicular to Pecan Street, also becomes full of cars and throngs of people walking up and down the major road.

In 2008 I attended the parade, which was set to start at 3:00 P.M. as usual. I arrived at 11:30 A.M., having been warned by a member of the Chamber of Commerce that parking would be challenging. By late morning, the side streets were already lined with parked cars. I circled the town a few times, looking for a spot to park, before squeezing my car into a space near the **Boley** Museum. Pecan Street was closed off to vehicles, and although the street was not yet full with spectators, people were milling about on foot and horseback. On a regular day, Pecan Street (pictured in chapter 3) appears deserted, but the rodeo weekend, and the parade in particular, transforms the entire town center. Along **Boley's** main drag were food trucks and eating stands, offering catfish sandwiches, pop (soda), ribs, brisket, and water.

Pecan Street during **Boley** Rodeo and Bar-B-Q Parade. Photo by author.

About two hours after I arrived, the event officially opened with two people perched on a stand with microphones, welcoming everyone to the **Boley** Rodeo and giving a speech about the town's history. The speech on this day was sometimes inaudible due to high winds and a barrage of sounds coming from Pecan Street. I stood right under the stand so I could hear the speech as well as possible, but in the background there were the clop of horses' hooves, revving motors, and radios blaring. Even though I suspect that most people could not hear him over the street noise, the narrator, a man appearing to be in his twenties and standing next to one of the elder town leaders, got out the following words:

> **[Boley]** became incorporated May 10th, 1905, as **Boley**, Indian Territory. Businesses were established. Houses were built. . . . Tim [*sic*] Haynes established the first Black church, the African Methodist Episcopal church, and built the first school in 1903. . . . To lure people to **Boley**, massive advertising campaigns were launched . . . promising freedom

from oppression for the Black man. It worked and they came in droves. . . . Their arrival was a cause for celebration with a gigantic rodeo. So it is fitting that on May 28th and 29th of 2008, **Boley** celebrates its 110th birthday party with a gigantic rodeo started in 190[5] and still carried on today. . . .

Unlike many neighboring towns, **Boley** did not fade entirely and cease to become a town. In the last few years, **Boley** has actually gained population. . . . **Boley** is a mecca for quiet country living. It is a good place to retire and take leave. **Boley** is steadily improving the quality of life for its inhabitants. It has walking paths and . . . the park has a pavilion, speakers, and a bandstand concession stand . . . complete with tables and charcoal. **Boley** has great plans for the future. It is grounded in the tourism business based on uniqueness as a nationally recognized historical Black town by Act of Congress in 1976. . . . It is home to the John Lilley Correctional Center and [Smokaroma], . . . invented by its founder, Maurice W. Lee senior, as son and grandson carry on the business even today.

Like the information in the rodeo program, the announcement over the loud-speaker emphasized **Boley's** successful Black past, which, in this narrative, was in part encouraged by its first rodeo. It is not surprising that the narrative highlights **Boley's** remarkable history at length. It also went on to boast of current institutions, including the prison, ending with the town's bright future. This is a promotional message in sync with the program's longer statement about **Boley's** new buildings and grants awarded to fund town projects, yet the souvenir program takes it even further by telling rodeo attendees to "Come and Stay."

The statements — both spoken and written — about **Boley's** present and future are essentially raceless and focused on the past. **Boley** is indeed described as a self-identified, historic Black town, and the history told about the rodeo and the community focuses on the town's Black population. However, what the town offers in the present is not race specific. The description of present town features that bode well for the town's future highlights resources and infrastructure for retirement and quiet living. For whom those features are well-suited, beyond retirement-age folks and people in search of quiet, is not specified. As such, **Boley** is described as a Black town open to anyone in search of a peaceful life.

The parade is never described in terms of race either. In fact, it is never described. It takes a decided backseat to the rodeo event in the material the town puts out. But the parade is nonetheless the major kickoff for the weekend and an important social space. It also clearly showcases blackness through its participants and what they represent. With the exception of a few White political candidates and members of a White Mennonite community, which exists within **Boley's** town limits,[10] those who march or ride in the parade are Black. Counting all the groups that paraded, I estimate that at last 65 to 70 percent represent Black-identified groups. Some come from **Boley** but most come from elsewhere: Oklahoma City, Tulsa, neighboring predominantly White communities like Okemah and Weewoka, and even Wichita, Kansas. They are steppers (dancers) from school and community clubs, Miss Black Teen Oklahoma, candidates for political office, Little Leaguers, bikers, cowboys, cowgirls, members of fraternal organizations, members of youth social groups, and students.

The parade groups represent a mix of connection and distinction: linked by their participation in a Black-town parade or by the type of group they represent, they are nonetheless distinguished by their group affiliation. And sometimes the distinctions are quite stark: the **Boley** Little Leaguers (a hometown group of young boys) versus lowriders (all young adult men, mostly from Oklahoma's major urban areas). Quite a few groups (the Black bikers and rider clubs), in fact, fit the latter demographic: young, urban Black males. Other groups represent older demographics and more established, national social groups, such as the Red Hats (a national women's social organization that is made up mostly of middle-aged women) and the Alaraf organization (a Black fraternal organization for adult men in Oklahoma City).

There is, then, an assortment of ages and social statuses among paraders that in other settings would be unlikely to join together. In fact, in Black towns you might hear some elders bemoan the lifestyle of Black youth, who they—the elders—believe do not uphold the historic decency of the community. I talked to some senior residents who lamented that young people in their community were partying publicly, drinking and playing music with cars moving all about the town streets late into the night. For today's elders, these sorts of activities depart from the more respectable social character of the Black towns that they say they knew and practiced in their youth.

In the parade, however, not only are young Black males included; symbols of the very lifestyle that some Black-town elders at times complain about are on full display alongside those of older paraders and very young paraders. The presence of the lowriders illustrates this facet. They cruise through the parade in their low-to-the-ground cars—tricked-out 1970s vehicles, like Chevy Impalas or Chryslers—in burnt-orange and metallic-yellow and

Fraternal organization from Oklahoma City marches in the **Boley** Rodeo and Bar-B-Q Parade. Photo by author.

sporting shiny rims. The cars usually contain at least two young men in the front seat and occasionally another in the back. The two in front might be leaning back in their seats, sometimes with doors wide open so that their full personae and the car's color-coordinated, immaculate interior is on display. Or they might sit outside the vehicle's windows, one leg leaning over the car door, as it drives slowly down the road. Hip-hop music blares from their cars, often with the bass turned so loud the thumping vibrates the street. Parades are generally noisy, but the arrival of the lowriders is especially unmistakable. The brilliance and loud beats of the cars broadcast their arrival. Unlike the Red Hats, who hold banners announcing their organization while smiling and waving at the crowds, the lowriders are expressionless and silent. They offer no sign or T-shirt to explain who they are. They don't throw candy out to children like the politicians and the women's organizations. Instead, they have a subdued, "cool pose," laid-back, as if the bright and loud cars are their animated arrival.

Lowriders in the **Boley** Rodeo and Bar-B-Q Parade. Photo by author.

Although usually associated with Los Angeles's Latinx community, low-rider culture is also popular among African American men, and Blacks were involved in the emergence of lowriding through Los Angeles car clubs.[11] Black lowriders are now found across the country and, stylistically, Black lowriding is distinct. It is associated with hip-hop culture and a "gangsta aesthetic" that you can see in hip-hop videos, hear in rap song lyrics, and find in iconic 1990s hip-hop films like *Boyz n the Hood*.[12] Sometimes cars are styled in ways that mirror images in hip-hop videos.[13] The use of the tricked-out car to present and style the self is also a way to perform physical and social mobility. By bringing their ostentatious vehicles into public view, lowriders across the country have "reimagined the [American] public landscape" in a way that elevates themselves,[14] centrally situating their aesthetic in contrast to the marginal space where their racialized communities are commonly placed. When Oklahoma's lowriders parade through **Boley's** streets in their brilliant and carefully designed autos, they contribute to this process of not merely elevating their status as Black men but also elevating Black culture

Lowriders in the **Boley** Rodeo and Bar-B-Q Parade. Photo by author.

more generally. The meanings they convey about Black social mobility—the arrival and prominence of a young, urban, Black-male aesthetic at the biggest Black-town event in the state—are brought into an event that puts Black culture broadly on display, doubling the efforts of the parade to carefully present a socially significant Black place.

Additionally, by being present in the parade, lowriders (as well as bikers and some of the horseback riding clubs) are part of the mix of blackness. The program and opening speech launching the parade tell about a community that was lifted through the activities and determination of hardworking Black people. It is now a quiet community suitable for retirement and peaceful living, spectators are told. The **Boley** Boy Scouts and Little Leaguers, the fraternal organizations and benevolent societies, the Red Hat society, and even the stepping clubs all fit this conventional image of Black respectability and social mobility. Lowriders and Black bikers do not. And yet, lowriders and Black bikers are not only *in* the parade; their presence is extensively interwoven with the more readily recognizable "respectable" groups that speak to **Boley's** presentation of self.

The parade, then, is an inclusive Black space that negotiates multiple Black identities. Lowriders and Little Leaguers alike are welcome *and* worthy of parading through the streets of a town that wants to present itself as the pinnacle of Black decency. Outside the parade, town elders may complain about young Black males whose aesthetic resembles that of the lowriders in the parade. Yet for the purposes of the parade and the town's biggest public event, diverse Black identities are included and profiled. In this way, the parade, and the larger rodeo event that is so important to **Boley's** image, allows for a representation of the complexities of blackness. Organizers of the event are open to displaying a broad swath of Black people, and groups like lowriders are willing to join in this Black experience that affirms their belonging.

In her book *Modern Blackness: Nationalism, Globalization, and the Politics of Culture in Jamaica*, Deborah A. Thomas describes a related dynamic in a Jamaican community in the late twentieth century. There, Black respectability associated with an older Black middle-class generation bumps up against the younger generation's notions and performance of a grittier blackness that is especially embodied by the scantily clad and bold dance-hall women DJs whom Thomas calls "ghetto feminists." Their "modern blackness" is public and plays a prominent role in defining Black Jamaican culture. The difference between ghetto feminists' and lowriders' challenge to Black respectability, however, is that the former wrestles with the older generation over appropriate blackness, while the latter shows less of a struggle *in the context of the parade*. The former, Thomas says, supplants the respectability associated with "creole nationalism," while Black-town respectability is not pushed out by lowriders' inclusion.[15] During and outside the rodeo weekend, there is indeed social separation between those embodying aspects of lowrider culture and the older generation town leadership steeped in middle-class respectability. But for the purposes of paraders who are permitted to be on full display as part of the town's showcasing events, lowriders are included, and I observed no clashes regarding their presence. In fact, the kinds of fluid interactions—neither starkly divided nor intimately intertwined across different socially defined groups—is reminiscent of what Mozell Hill described about class structure in mid-twentieth-century Black towns. Hill found that there was mobility and flexibility across class boundaries due to a common purpose around race and community.[16]

Boley organizers of the rodeo celebration are not alone in including low-riders in the town parade. I went to several Black-town parades, and lowriders were always included in the mix. They have paraded through **Taft** and **Langston** as well as towns with sizeable Black communities like Arcadia and Okmulgee. In fact, the same lowriders whom I saw in **Boley's** parade appeared in most others that I attended. They do the circuit of Black-town events as do other social groups. Thus, Black towns use parades to publicly embrace a broad understanding of blackness and to publicly present a diverse Black community. This is in keeping with other Black parades—most notably New Orleans's second line parades—that use celebratory processions to bring blackness into public view and display community in a way that departs from more conventional experiences of Black marginalization.[17] Because the **Boley** Rodeo Parade occurs in a Black-town space and not a broader public space—such as with second line parades, where largely dispossessed, socially and economically marginalized African Americans use the city's well-trodden thoroughfares to claim space and become "owners of the streets"[18]—participants are claiming a space that is already seen as a "Black space." However, they are using that existing Black space, where thousands of people converge for a weekend, to openly present and celebrate blackness in a way that demonstrates inclusion. Black people who participate in the parade are able to join in this celebration and public display. Indeed, by advertising the event widely and holding it on such a large scale, the event organizers broaden the Black-town space, making it a public Black space. This is the converse of the tours that lift Black towns out of their marginal location by connecting them to prominent centers in Oklahoma. The rodeo event brings those centers into the Black town as people from the state's major cities and beyond converge in the space. The rodeo—particularly the parade—offers people from those centers an image of blackness that, on the one hand, affirms Black respectability but, on the other, negotiates traditional Black respectability with a more expansive and complex rendering of blackness.

I left the rodeo arena at 10:00 P.M. By then, Pecan Street was quieter, and the bustle of the day had moved to the stands of the rodeo arena, where visitors congregated to watch Black cowboys perform their sport. The rodeo is a more raucous activity compared to the parade, and things were still going strong late into the night. As I was leaving, people were still arriving. I reached my car more easily than I had found a parking space in the morning. I drove down Pecan Street and turned left on Highway 62. There were still many cars parked alongside the road and young people, seemingly socializing, walking up and down the highway. I noticed helicopters beaming lights down onto the road and scanning a wooded area far off the shoulder—ironically, the kind of well-known imagery from *Boyz n the Hood*, with urban Black men who roll in their lowriders while commenting on police surveillance of their community. I drove out of town, thinking about **Boley** and its Black identity, noting the line of police along Highway 62 and the John Lilley Correctional Facility across the road, a few feet down from the turnoff to Pecan Street, where Black people had just offered their community as a peaceful, inclusive, fun, and contemporary Black place.

Dana Comes Home

Many people who go to the **Boley** Rodeo have been living away and return for the event because **Boley** is home. One person I saw in the parade had a large placard on his snazzy sports car: "Home Town Boley; Now Wichita, Kansas." In fact, for many people a sense of home is what makes a Black town matter and is their pull to return. We think of this sentiment fitting people who grew up in the place. Most Black towners would say that about the town they call home. But Dana Armstrong is different. A woman in her early fifties, she had lived in Promise for only four years when I first met her, and yet she told me she was drawn to Promise because it is home.

I spoke with her in her trailer—or "manufactured house," as she said her cousin calls it—relatively far from the center of Promise but not as far as the next town. To find her, I had to follow her detailed directions and caveats about turns and twists and roads I might encounter that were not really roads. When I arrived, I told her she was right. I almost missed her house a few times, unsure if I was headed in the right direction. But once I arrived I clearly saw two perpendicular trailer homes on an open lot. The one facing me horizontally was hers; I would later discover that the one to my right that stretched vertically was her daughter's.

There was no sign of anyone when I first pulled up to the lot, but once I knocked on the door I could see that Dana was waiting for me. She has a subdued demeanor, but I could still tell that she was excited for my visit. The house looked very tidy, and she had a stack of photo albums out on the table that I figured she had placed there in anticipation of my arrival. Like so many other people, she assumed that I wanted to know about Black-town history. Those albums contained her family history, and they were all about why she came to Promise.

Dana said she chose to live in Promise after she faced a decision: whether to move to rural Mississippi or to Promise, both places where she had inherited land belonging to her extended family. Promise won out because it felt like "home and history," she said. The statement could jar someone who heard the places that stamped Dana's life history. An aptly self-described "city girl" who had never lived in a rural area, she was born in Kansas City, Missouri, lived for most of her childhood in St. Louis, and then for seventeen years of her adult life resided in Dallas. It's true that for about seven years, as a child, she spent summers in Promise, visiting her great-grandmother. For those seven years, Dana would come with her family to spend several weeks with Grandma Alice. Childhood memories of the visits are part of the reason why Promise had a homelike feeling for Dana.

The ease of her present-day connections in the town also contribute to that feeling. "Everyone here [in Promise] is family," Dana said, stressing the few degrees of separation among Promise folk. The point was nicely illustrated when she mentioned her encounter with an older woman in the town, Ms. Crandall. Dana said Ms. Crandall doesn't remember Dana's name, but calls out to her every time she sees her: "Aren't you one of the Armstrong girls?" To which Dana said she dutifully replies, "Yes, ma'am." "You know you're supposed to be going to Promise Baptist Church," Ms. Crandall retorted, making Dana laugh when she told me the story. "And every time she sees me she reminds me that [Promise Baptist] is still down there, and I keep saying, 'Yes, ma'am.'" Ms. Crandall seemed to equate Dana's family with the church and was reminding her about going to Promise Baptist, as if that is where she belongs.

The other part that made Promise "home and history" for Dana were the family reunions that her extended family held, sometimes in Promise, sometimes elsewhere, but all with a connection to Promise. I learned about the reunions as she leafed through the photos and a family-history booklet that she had set out on the table in anticipation of my visit. She had been telling me about a church in Promise that her extended family belonged to, and as I was asking questions about their relationship to the church, she abruptly grabbed the photo album and started naming people in the pictures. I could tell that she was eager to share them with me, especially since there was little segue from our discussion to the photos. "That's my cousin, Otis," she said. "He died . . . last year. . . . This is Aunt Tiny. She's ninety-something. Still smoking three packs a day." As we flipped through the album pages she went on to point out Aunt Linda, Aunt Marion, and Aunt Stacy, telling me a bit about each of their lives. The photo album, styled almost like a scrapbook, was mostly images with some captions and short paragraphs about each person or the larger families. As she would call them out she identified people by their relationship to her as well as by their family surname — the Armstrongs, the Painters, and others.

We looked over her family booklet and photos, with Dana narrating the pages in detail, much like a family genealogy session. The anthropologist in me was wowed by what was essentially a six-page kinship chart of the family from the 1890s to 2005 contained inside the extensive reunion booklet. Lucille and Arthur Armstrong, Dana's great-grandparents and the matriarch and patriarch of the extended family, are profiled as the origin of the family chart. They were married in 1905 in a small Oklahoma town. In 1915 they settled a mile outside Promise, renting a 160-acre farm, where they grew crops and raised small livestock. Although nine years after their wedding Arthur died of an illness, they had ten children in that time period and went on to have nine grandchildren who became the basis for future family gatherings. Years after Arthur's death, Lucille bought forty-eight acres in Promise, which she farmed with her children for twenty years. After that, she moved to a Midwestern city while maintaining ownership of her home in Promise, leaving the family connected to the town.

The reunions to celebrate Lucille, Arthur, and their descendants began in 1974 and averaged two per decade. Two were held in Promise, while the rest were spread out across the Midwest and Far West, where different family members lived, indicating the mobility of Black-town families but also the Black town as an anchor. Dana attended many of these reunions that told the story of Lucille and Arthur's success in raising a family through their hard work in the surrounds of Promise. This narrative, repeated over and over again, surely helped Dana think of Promise as home. It was clear that many of her extended family had lived in Promise and that Lucille's and Arthur's lives in the town were the starting point of the family story. And in showing me the reunion booklet, Dana often pointed out the family connection to Promise, making clear to me that Promise was a focal point for the family. Within the booklet, "THE JOURNEY HOME" was scrawled across a divider sheet in large type, with a map of Promise in the lower left corner.

The pages in the booklet showed a layout of the family's burial plots, naming the placement of each family member along with the date of their "departure." The reunion was a way to bring family together, but it was also a way to honor and remember those who had passed. Indeed, the reunion booklet is replete with accounts of people's memories of their kin who are no longer living, especially Arthur and Lucille, who receive a five-page "biographical portrait" of their lives.

It is interesting that one impetus for Dana choosing Promise is the family reunions that, in addition to her childhood visits, helped her learn about her family connection to Promise. Family reunions are especially active ritual events among African Americans, serving to connect Black families separated by migration and enslavement.[19] They also connect families across generations, affirming the value of elder knowledge and teaching younger members about family rituals and culture.[20] A primary source of Dana's connection to her Promise family and roots was the reunions that contributed to her considering the town home. Although Dana is three generations removed from Arthur and Lucille and has not had any physical ties or visits to Promise since age fourteen, she was the only heir to Grandma Alice's land who chose to move there. The continued connections to her kin through the reunions certainly helped motivate her to make the move. The reunion material and ritual gatherings tell the story of a family not only anchored to Promise but successful through Promise. And the ties that have been kept up through regular family gatherings in Promise — gatherings in which the family history is narrated — also mattered to Dana's decision to settle there.

Among her family members, Dana was unusual in this regard. As she described it, most of her family did not have any interest in the land. "Some family [don't] care," she said. "They don't want to fool with it. As far as they were concerned, whoever's out here [such as Dana], they can have it." She pointed out other tracts of land nearby that are also family property. "My mother's oldest sister, Mother Lucy, . . . owns some of it, and then when the land was divided up when my great-grandmother died, and then divided up again later as older members of the family died, the land across the road went to Mother Lucy's kids."

To claim the abandoned property meant that Dana had to clear the land, which she described as an arduous process that both she and her daughter managed on their own. It is so arduous that few return to do what Dana did. Abandoned family land is one of the big challenges to Black-town leadership in all the Black towns I studied. Mayors talk about strategies to get people to clean up their land, but I mostly heard of such strategies not working. It was a major undertaking for Dana and her daughter:

We came out here with two lawnmowers, plain push lawnmowers, a couple of weed eaters, a handful of friends, a small chainsaw, and cleared off as best we could. [We] cleared off just enough to get [my daughter's home] out here and set up, so . . . when her house got moved out here it was a lot more wooded. All of that in front except for the driveway was . . . weeds and trees as thick as that across the road. . . . So you couldn't see the front of his house. We had to make a path from the back door to the front door. . . . And it took a little while, and then this was the next closest clear spot that was close to the road, so we worked on clearing this out, and once again trees was all the way up within that much of the back. . . . We had to clear out land to put my septic tank back there. That over there where it's cut down there, kind of like the front? Okay. That was kind of clear, but that's because one of my uncles came out and put that shed up because he said he was going to move down here, and of course he changed his mind. [Laughs.] So that part was a little bit cleared. Uh, but all of this out here, no, it was completely overgrown. . . . So it's going to take us like forever.

Dana seemed ready for the long haul, and it appeared to me that she had hunkered down in Promise. She joined the Promise Town Council and seemed invested in working on the town (including getting other families to clean up their lots). She continued to go to church outside Promise, and she admitted that her social network was mostly family and friends who are not in the town. But in this way she is not different from people who have been longtime residents of their Black town. Social connections and networks are spread widely—within and beyond the town—for Black-town residents.

I asked Dana my usual question about whether she considers the town she lives in as Black. She was unequivocal. Yes, it is, she said. She stressed that it is *historically* Black. She was okay with Whites moving in, and like other Black towners she thought that building up the town will require having more Whites move there. Also like others, Dana was trying to work out her thinking on the subject. She told me that sometimes she thinks the overgrown weeds will deter Whites, which seemed to make her delight in the thought. But then she said that the town needs Whites to move in, so deterring them is not a good idea. Still, it did not seem to make her think that Whites in Black towns would change things: "No matter who moves in, it's going to always be a historically Black town." And for her—as far as I could tell based on our conversation—it's always going to be home.

For the Culture?

Asha had fewer ties to Wrightsville than Dana had to Promise. She had no family in a Black town and had not visited one before she encountered Wrightsville. Originally from the East Coast, she was in Oklahoma attending college when, one day, someone in a university office saw her looking forlorn. The person inquired about her, and she said she was not sure what she would be doing after she finished school. The university staff person invited her to join a group that he thought she would like. Getting connected with the group set her on a path that led to her taking up residence in Wrightsville, and she had been there ever since.

I learned this story talking to Asha in her house. I met her there after a born-and-raised Wrightsvillian told me they thought she would be an interesting person for me to talk to since she had moved there from elsewhere. I went over to her house right away, and after giving my usual introduction I asked if I could interview her at another time. Our interaction seemed unremarkable: she was receptive, and we made a tentative plan to meet up. However, a few hours later, she called me, sounding as if the matter was urgent. She apologized for not being more open to my visit when I stopped by, which I found odd since I had not perceived her as unwilling. She was eager to set up the interview and told me that the man responsible for urging her to move to Wrightsville—a man leading the group she joined after college—encouraged her to call me back quickly once she told him about my visit to her house.

There are other Blacks who move to a Black town fairly abruptly or outside of a long-range plan (such as retirement). Most are like Dana or others who have some type of family experience that draws them to Black towns. Few are like Asha. After joining the group that she found, Asha's calling was participating in a project to support Black self-esteem and better Black-White race relations. The project was led by a man named Dr. K, who is based in the Southeast and has a national following, with chapters across the country advancing his work. Asha was one of his devotees. She was so invested in his work that she hunkered down in Wrightsville to further the effort.

As I understood Dr. K's work from Asha's explanation, it is a plan to improve society by putting together the mission of Martin Luther King and Thomas Jefferson. From King's work on racial integration and Jefferson's ideas outlined in the Declaration of Independence, Dr. K developed a scientific method for bringing the men's purpose into action. Asha said he calls that process "Self and Humanity," a science for assessing and gaining an understanding of the self, to be the kind of person who lives out King's and Jefferson's ideals. According to her, Dr. K believes that we need to get back in touch with our highest potential as it exists at birth but that we have lost along the way. As Asha stated it, "The only way a person can come to the fullness of understand[ing] a self is to identify who she/he is at conception. . . . [T]he capacity of each baby in that mother's womb is the same. . . . [E]ven though he was in an environment of slavery, [Jefferson] knew that all men were created equal. . . . Dr. K took it to the next level to fit twenty-first-century language, and he said all *Homo sapien* babies are born the same." Earlier in our conversation, Asha explained why Martin Luther King was also important to Dr. K's work.

> Dr. King wanted all people to get along, African Americans —. He was not only for us, he was for European Americans. . . . He specifically stated in his speech that he had a dream that his little children would not be judged by the color of their skin but by the content of their character, and . . . we remain isolated, don't have a clue on how to come together and make economic development work, . . . so much division it is just —. . . . Dr. K said people have not lived . . . out [King's dream] because they don't know how to live it out. . . . When Dr. King got killed . . . [Dr. K] said we don't have a leader now. What are we going to do? . . . And so he began to search, trying to find somebody that would take Dr. King's place.

Dr. K is that leader, picking up where King left off, developing a science to enable the individual to realize their potential and achieve equality of the races. His science is what brought Asha to Wrightsville. She was there to work with town youth, teaching them about themselves by using Dr. K's method. For five years, she taught community classes with teens, leading them in personality self-assessments and in assignments to help them discover their biases and understand themselves. The instrument she used for this, the Tennessee Self-Concept Scale, is a known self-worth assessment tool in psychology, developed in 1956. Participants taking the Self and Humanity course respond to questions about how they think about themselves, how they interact with friends, and how they sleep. This approach to engendering racial equality is not a systems analysis to understand how people are situated in a society; rather, it centers on the individual. In that way, it was not like today's popular diversity trainings that also purport to promote and facilitate social equity. Instead, Dr. K's model, carried out by Asha, worked on teaching the individual about themselves, boosting their sense of self-worth, and thereby building up their potential to live life as an equal participant in society. Achieving that meant living out King's and Jefferson's ideals. Dr. K was making that happen.

Interestingly, in the 1940s Mozell C. Hill also conducted a survey of Blacktown youth that assessed their racial self-esteem.[21] However, Hill's purpose was different. He wanted to compare the perspectives of youth in Black towns with those in more racially diverse communities, which sociologist Charles Johnson had famously studied.[22] Comparing Johnson's results for a "mixed race" community in the rural South with the results Hill obtained from applying the same scale, the Race Attitude Test, in Oklahoma Black towns, Hill set out to assess whether a town's racial composition and regional location influenced Black residents' views of Whites. While his results did not show drastic differences between the two communities' views on a variety of levels, his interesting finding was that Black town youth exhibited far stronger and more positive self-perceptions and views of Blacks than those in Johnson's study. Hill concluded his overall work on the Black towns by asserting that, when Blacks are not "under the pressure of the dominant White society, there is a relaxation of racial tension."[23]

Asha and Dr. K would probably conclude the opposite about what was going on in Wrightsville in the early 2000s, while Asha was there. One of Dr. K's premises is that people of African descent have not freed themselves from the legacies of enslavement. That is why they have not achieved their fullest potential. They have what Asha repeatedly referred to as a "slave mentality," again signaling the individual perspective. Slavery was "the most brutal thing that could happen to us as a people," she said. "Even though people will say, 'Well, other people were in slavery,' nobody was taken from their land but us." In Asha's view, few people have freed themselves from the impact of this experience, but Dr. K was an example of someone who had. He and his followers also believed they were able to work with individuals through the classes, instructing people on self-awareness and how to surmount the impact of enslavement, thereby "freeing themselves."

Wrightsville was selected as a site for Dr. K's work because of his emphasis on developing a positive self-concept among people who have not achieved freedom. I suspect that, as a Black town with a majority African American population, Wrightsville was ripe for the project. Asha felt that Wrightsvillians fit the description of people who had not extracted themselves from enslavement. However, instead of race being the reason, she pointed to the community's rurality and economic fragility. For her, if a community had achieved its fullest potential and lived out King's and Jefferson's ideals, its populace would be in better shape economically, and they would be living equally to others in better-resourced communities. She was frustrated that Wrightsville had not reached this point and that her work with youth had been stalled when she lost access to the space for holding her classes.

Although Asha clearly was a devotee of Dr. K and was carrying out his work, a question remains about whether that work was also "for the culture," as the saying goes. That is, was Dr. K's project for uplifting and supporting "the [Black] race"? Dr. K's model was about race relations and achieving racial unity. According to Asha, he believed that most people—regardless of race—had not freed themselves from the legacy of enslavement, and his science was meant to be applicable to all people. European Americans and African Americans alike—the two groups she mentioned—were both negatively impacted by the history, so both needed freeing. In fact, Asha said a few White youth took her classes after Wrightsville Black youth invited them, and Asha welcomed their participation. However, it was hard not to consider Asha's self-presentation: both times I saw her she was dressed in African garb (a caftan and headwrap made of African print), and her home had other décor that seemed symbolic of Africa. Asha also repeatedly referred to the impact of slavery on "us" in ways that did not sound like "us" as a nation but rather "us" as a race. When she said, "Nobody was taken from their land but us," I took her to mean "us Black people" or, as she and Dr. K preferred, "African Americans." Moreover, the siting of the project in a Black town and working predominantly with Black youth on their self-esteem seemed an investment in building up a Black community and the Black people in it, helping them to "free themselves," as Dr. K had.

Unlike tourism packages, community development organizers, and rodeo programs, Asha was not looking to Black towns as sites of greatness to be held up and revered. She did not talk a lot about the successful Black-town past. For Asha (working through Dr. K), Black greatness needed to be cultivated—scientifically—in Wrightsville, no matter its history.

The Appeal of Community

When people first started moving to Black towns in the nineteenth century, community and race were among the motivators. Personal safety and economic security were certainly draws, but we would be wrong to ignore that being part of a community of other Black people was significant. The collective experience was a bonus.

The people who are moving into Black towns in the twenty-first century and the people who are coming to participate deeply in Black-town events are coming, in part, for the collective Black experience and, in the case of the rodeo, the public Black experience. Clearly, unlike for Whites as developers or new residents, economics is not a motivator as much as is the social dimension of the move or deep participation in Black-town life. That social dimension often—typically—includes participating in community rituals and connecting with community members. Rodeo parade participants, Dana, and Asha all felt or exhibited some kind of connection to the Black towns they came to. Those connections are about family, Black culture, and Black self-esteem. The blackness of Black towns, the blackness of the population, and Black-town rituals are part of what fuel and motivate these connections.

However, community is as much about relationships and connections as it is about disjuncture.[24] As much as we like to romanticize "community" as synonymous with "harmony," community involves negotiating these disjunctures. In Dana's story, social divisions were less apparent, but they are clear in Asha's story as well as in the rodeo parade. As the most glaring case, Asha's notion of what the Black community of Wrightsville prioritizes did not fit with her purpose for moving there. She had an idea of the community as an ideal space for promoting racial equality, and she was drawn to it for that purpose, even though her work ultimately did not advance as she hoped. Differently, the parade is a display of diverse "blacknesses," lined up separately but grouped together in the event. The groups work out their disjunctures for the purposes of the parade and perhaps for the benefit of the public presentation of a Black town. In the end, however, all of the individuals and groups profiled in this chapter are drawn to Black towns because of some feature of the towns' Black identity, whether as a rich and active Black celebration space, a place with deep Black family roots, or a place where Black people are still carrying and limited by the impact of enslavement. They all inserted themselves into Black-town life, navigating the allure of Black community and contending with its complexities.

CHAPTER FIVE

The Appeal of a Black Place

The late geographer Harold Rose was a pioneer in conceptualizing Black towns. In 1965 he outlined a definition of Black towns in which the criteria included the towns having a rural location, a nonblack population of no more than 1 percent, and limited economic dependence on other incorporated communities (regardless of race) with the towns controlling their own political governance. Black towns that met the first two criteria but are political and physical appendages of other communities were not, for Rose, Black towns. Thus, he placed importance on Black towns' political independence, suggesting emphasis on self-determination. But, significantly, his definition allowed for communities being connected to other places.[1]

While disagreeing with some of the parameters of Black-town connections, other researchers coming up with a typology or definition of Black towns have also looked at Black-town linkages. Sundiata Cha-Jua explored the transition in an Illinois Black town's status, a transition that included periods of political dependence on neighboring communities (and thus, Cha-Jua disagreed with Rose's exclusion of political dependency).[2] Andrew Wiese argued that Black towns are not only rural but also in the suburbs, to the extent that suburban Black communities have defined geographic boundaries and are Black-identified. For Wiese, rurality is not a necessary criterion to define a Black town, because Black communities in the suburbs reflect similar aspirations that led to the formation of rural Black towns. In all of these examples, Black towns are conceptualized as interwoven with diverse places and spaces that vary by race, economics, political status, and geography.[3] While specific and different from one another, these theories of Black towns argue for a broad understanding of Black-town boundaries and features. The theories relate to other arguments about blackness and place-making or space-making as being other than physical boundedness.[4] Those ideas are about the mobility, porosity, dynamism, and connections that make up a Black town, but also the centrality and modernity of those towns—all features, I argue, that make Black towns appealing places.

As seen through Black towns, a Black sense of place or a Black imaginary of space is an idea of place where Black greatness is respected as central to the American story. It is a space that is inclusive, economically vibrant, and socially engaged—that is, committed to Black community. It is also a space where people of African descent are centered, if not the numerical majority. It is where Black people have made their mark and are recognized for their worth. Its borders are porous enough to allow for inclusion of a variety of people, expanding possibilities, opening up opportunities, and leveraging claims and narratives that reposition Black people out from the margins of society. It is important to underscore that the Black-town reality is more than the Black imaginary of itself, but that does not impede the Black ideal of the space. Economic possibilities may be limited. Social interactions and uses of Black towns may be unequal. But the imaginary of that space transcends those experiences.

History is important to the Black sense of a Black town. Black towns appeal in part because of their history, from which can be mobilized a range of narratives and demonstrations that tell of and support this Black sense of place. Interestingly, when I began my research, I was intent on studying contemporary Black towns and moving away from the work of historians. I resisted studying Black-town history. I felt certain that the story of the Black-town past had been told so well and so often by historians, and that Black towns warranted a story about their present. I wanted to contribute a new perspective on Black towns. As a cultural anthropologist who studies present-day rural communities, I considered myself prepared to research what Black-town life means and is in the twenty-first century, especially the realities of race in that space. And yet, my research has shown that history is vital to today's Black-town story and the imagination of Black towns as Black places. It is not *just* that telling about what happened in Black towns one hundred years ago is important to preserve the historic record. Black-town history is critical to the contemporary political work that people with connections in Black towns and people living in Black towns are doing in support of the towns and Black Americans more generally. This is work that includes presenting a case about the merit of Black towns and, more broadly, the economic, social, and cultural value of Black people and Black places to their communities as well as to the nation. In many ways, these arguments are in sync with the well-known arguments emerging out of recent efforts like the Movement for Black Lives, in which asserting the worth of Black life and demanding the valuing of Black life is primary. Telling the Black-town-history story and locating it centrally in major themes of the country, I believe, is part of asserting that worth and making those demands, as a present-day project.

There is a double side to Black towns' appeal. Besides the attraction of accounts about historic Black greatness, Black towns are alluring because of their present fragility, particularly their infrastructural and economic fragility. On the one hand, being precarious makes them appealing to developers and absentee land buyers who can profit from the vulnerability of a rural Black town. This is not new for Black places. Black towns' material fragility makes them susceptible to rural versions of gentrification and state development schemes that are rarely tuned in to a Black imaginary of space. On the other hand, the economically and infrastructurally fragile Black town is appealing to those who want to chart alternative and better futures for Black people, and thereby demonstrate the value of Black community. Black towns are like countless Black communities, then—urban, rural, and otherwise—negotiating material fragility with capitalist ventures (large and small) that threaten to displace Black people from their own property. Or they are digging in to conceive and dream of a different economic reality.

This leads me to conclude that the racialization of space[5]—a concept that has received much attention for explaining the social, economic, and geographic location and experience of communities of color—does not fully explain Black towns. Yes, Black places are linked, for example, to prison sitings, gentrification, loss of local schools, occupational vulnerability, and more. They are subject to spatial violence that causes the communities social and economic harm. However, while Black towns are precarious and marginal spaces that can be discounted, dismissed, and even assaulted for their blackness, economic status, and rurality, they are simultaneously upheld and centered. Ideas about their cultural significance bring them prominence. But Black towns are also repositioned from the margins due to the work that various people and institutions put in to render the communities significant. They are repositioned because of the narratives people and institutions display about them that attract interest. Black towns, therefore, sit at the nexus of the racialization of space and the appeal of a Black place. The nexus is important, which leaves one critical takeaway: to talk about a successful Black place does not have to mean only talking about the triumphs and the achievements to the exclusion of the challenges. We can witness Black historic achievements as well as current community efforts to uphold and enact social equality and inclusion, modern living, and academic and occupational achievement while also acknowledging fractures. Experiencing marginality does not foreclose success, and experiencing extensive success does not exclude being marginalized. The composite picture of lives connected to Black towns demonstrates this.

What we can also take away from Black towns (particularly when considering how the communities negotiate economic fragility and social marginality) is that place—the Black town—is a site for rallying around blackness. It is a space for analyzing and redefining Black people's existence. Black towners and others who are attracted to the communities find ways to memorialize Black community (and by extension Black life), make and remake it, guard it, and celebrate it. They do so by hunkering down in Black towns as well as by pulling from Black-town experiences, past and present, inclusive but not exclusive of spatial violence.

Appealing to Me

I should probably include myself here. Eighty years after my great-uncle—Uncle Buddy—set out for Oklahoma, fleeing from the barber that "ran him out of Alabama," I went to the state for the first time to begin my research. And, of course, I went straight to **Boley**. Just like most people do. I turned off Route 62 onto Pecan Street. I was struck by how the street that had boasted the sixty-plus businesses detailed in my grandfather's dissertation was now a wide and long stretch of boarded-up buildings. I admit that I had a thought about a tumbleweed rolling down that road toward my car because, at first glance, the street felt barren. I saw the **Boley** Community Center with a few cars parked outside. I entered the door and introduced myself to someone sitting at a table where the senior citizen's lunch usually takes place. I started telling that person about my research interests. About my grandfather's research decades ago. About how my mother spent her childhood years in **Langston**. The person was expressionless. She even struck me as unimpressed. I became sure of my suspicion when she asked, "And where's your mother *now*?" in a tone that made me think she questioned the commitment of my mother—a Black-town migrant who spent her adult life elsewhere—to the place I was now claiming as my family roots.

Through the course of my research I learned that people like me—descendants of former Black-town residents—are also a "Black-town type." We are the people in search of family origins, maybe wanting to make a documentary or write a book about the towns. We are the Black people who maybe want to buy some land and get away from the big city, or who think that Black towns are going to be a bastion of remarkable Black communalism. We think they are going to be a "quiet gold mine," as a man once referred to them when he asked me for an interview.

I have interviewed numerous people who find Black towns appealing and are drawn to them. Yet even if I would distinguish myself from others, the **Boley** resident at the community center had seen so many of me. And, yes, she was unimpressed by the ways that we imagined Black towns as spaces that can do racially and socially unique things. The allure of Black towns con-

Letchen Hill's grave at **Boley** Elementary School. Photo by author.

tinues to prompt diverse sorts of twenty-first-century migrations—including my own—all connected somehow to the idea of exceptional places, but as the numbers of these "migrants" swell, the allure represents an increasingly common pattern.

When I told the person in the community center that my Uncle Buddy also had lived in **Boley**, she asked his name. She became more interested and said she knew him. She told me he was buried near the school—what would become the last Black-town school to close its doors a few years after I arrived in Oklahoma. I got in my car to find a cemetery near the school to see his grave. I circled around and around looking for it, without success. A man mowing the school lawn stopped and asked me what I was searching for. I explained. He said to me, "There isn't a cemetery over here. What's your uncle's name?" "Letchen Hill," I replied. At that, he motioned me over to the school lawn, and there, alongside the walkway leading to the school's front door, lay my uncle's headstone, the lone burial plot at that location. I snapped a picture. I look at the photo every so often. It reminds me of how my research journey began—with a family "discovery" and story. It reminds me what first drew me to Black towns.

Epilogue

Precarity in the Post-Obama Era

I ended my research in 2012, but of course life in Black towns continued on. From media stories and news that I heard by word of mouth, my sense was that economic and infrastructural fragility and Black towners' efforts to address them remain. I'm not aware of any new stores popping up or major rural employers for Black-town residents. In 2014, I learned that the small Black town of **Tullahassee**, Oklahoma, was experiencing a water crisis. The town had an unpaid $30,000 water bill to the neighboring, predominantly White town of Porter, which supplies **Tullahassee** (and other rural towns, Black and non-Black) with the resource. (Other Black towns have similar arrangements with their neighboring cities.) Dependency on White towns for critical infrastructure is apparently common among Black towns across the country and is known to cause vulnerability.[1] And during my research I observed deep discussions about Black-town water situations — the importance of the revenue for town economies, the fragile state of town water facilities, and residents' questions about high water bills. **Tullahassee** faced losing its water supply if the bill was not paid to Porter. In the stories that I read, **Tullahasse's** leadership and residents were worried. Some questioned where the money that residents had paid toward their water bills had gone, while others expressed concern that their bills had increased astronomically. Most just worried about the town's future.[2] Residents went online to crowdsource-fund the issue. They took out a page with the heading "Help Save Tullahassee" to try to raise money and ensure the town's existence, just like Mrs. Hanson, Celia, and others have worked to save their towns. The case went into litigation, and, the last I heard, in 2017, it was not resolved. **Tullahassee** still had its water, although Porter's leadership said they could cut the water off at any moment, and new residents were prohibited from getting water connections.[3]

The water crisis in **Tullahassee** speaks to the ongoing insufficiency of Black-town infrastructure, whether for economic activity or public utilities. There have been other environmental crises as well. In Oklahoma, fracking began in 2010, and the environmental fallout was most apparent with earthquakes that started occurring in 2012, especially in central Oklahoma, where **Boley** sits. Indeed, **Boley** has often been in the news as a place impacted by the earthquakes.[4]

History Still Matters

The notion of Black towns in peril was captured in a NewsOk.com series called "Endangered Black History."[5] The story profiled six Black communities in Oklahoma, two of which are Black towns. **Boley** and **Langston** were included. Despite the title, the hook of the series was the rich history of the communities. For **Langston** and **Boley**, it tells the appealing story of Black-town history, that is, the story of Black social and economic success in the early twentieth century. That narrative is set against the present material struggles, although the present received far less attention in the articles.

The narrative of the Black-town-history success story still appears to resonate. In fact, it seems to me that there has been a rise in national coverage of Black-town history. Several major news outlets have published pieces about Oklahoma's towns. Additionally, journalism professor Kari Barber produced the film *Struggle and Hope*, which helped bring broader attention to Oklahoma's towns.[6] The documentary was one of the first comprehensive films on Oklahoma's Black towns that looked at both the past and the present. Further, the broad story of thriving and economically sophisticated Black communities that we heard on the bus tours (discussed in chapter 2) made its way to the Smithsonian's National Museum of African American History and Culture, which opened in 2016. The footage we viewed of small-city Oklahoma Blacks living their sophisticated lives became part of the Smithsonian's collections.[7]

Tourism of Black towns in Oklahoma has grown since 2012. A new, small, Black-run organization, the Coltrane Group, has begun tours and exhibits, expanding Black-town-history tours in the state and bringing the private sector to heritage tours of Black towns. Additionally, a new visitor center for Honey Springs Battlefield moved from its remote location on the battlefield trails to the center of town in **Rentiesville**. From my perspective, this gives **Rentiesville** a chance for new tourist activity within its borders (in addition to the Dusk 'til Dawn Festival). It also repositions Honey Springs more prominently in a Black town, threading a little more closely Black Americans with prominent national history.

Whitening of Black Towns?

While I still caution against relying on census data to depict who makes up Black towns, I found myself looking at estimates for Black-town demographics in 2017. Recall that several Black towns saw a slight increase in the White population between 2000 and 2010. I wondered, is this a trend that is continuing? According to census estimates, which rely on birth, death, and migration records, it is. All except two Black towns show an increase in their White population for the six-year period, 2011–2017. Some increases are substantial, as much as 36 percent.[8] If these estimates bear out in 2020, Black towns—amid (or perhaps because of) their infrastructural, environmental, and economic fragility—may still appeal (and perhaps increasingly so) to Whites as residential places.

However, even with the possibility of a major shift in a town's racial demographics, it is hard to imagine that Black towns would lose their significant racial identifiers this soon. Tourism of Black towns continues to expand with a branding of the communities as Black towns. Events like the **Boley** Rodeo and the **Rentiesville** Dusk 'til Dawn Blues Festival, packaged as African American cultural events, continue to draw crowds. At the same time, significant and ongoing changes in Black towns' racial demographics could mean struggles over their identity, much as Mieka Polanco documented in a rural Virginia town whose residents were divided over whether and how to present just what "historically Black" meant to their community.[9]

Race and Rural America in the Trump Era

We've heard so much about rural America since the 2016 presidential election, especially how rural Whites are responsible for Donald Trump's win. Oklahoma, a largely rural state, has been a red state for presidential elections going back almost to the 1960s. Yet the precinct-level data for 2016 show a more nuanced story. It is true that few in rural Oklahoma voted non-Republican in 2016, but five (out of hundreds of) rural precincts did.[10] Four of those five are Black communities: **Boley**, **Langston**, **Taft**, and **Fort Coffee**. The latter, another predominantly Black community that has a large Freedmen population, is not classified as a Black town but has some resonance with the Black-town story in terms of aspects of its history.[11] Anadarko, a Native American small city with a population just over six thousand, is the fifth rural precinct that carried Hillary Clinton.

Black-town precinct election results are a minuscule portion of Oklahoma's rural voter landscape, but they are still a reminder that rural America is not homogenous. Our perception that rural America is responsible for the extreme conservative and racist values that have been more boldly on display since 2016 does not capture the complexity of what goes on in rural areas. Oklahoma is also an extreme case in terms of how underrepresented rural Blacks are. Rural blacks in Appalachia, the Mississippi Delta, and the "Black Belt" of the Deep South have a higher representation in those regions, where support for Trump was not strong or uniform.[12] A more complex picture of rural America that takes into account racial and ethnic diversity is necessary. As Mara Casey Tieken says, rural Black America has a "different history from rural White America; a history of forced migration, enslavement, and conquest. . . . [Black] rural America receives . . . lower pay and fewer protections for its labor."[13] Thus, even with the economic precariousness that connects Blacks and Whites in rural communities across the country, the difference in political behavior throws into question the merits of a strict economic calculus to explain why we saw overwhelming rural support for Trump and, ultimately, what rural America is about. Black towns are especially instructive for helping us break the myth.

Notes

Preface

1. **Guthrie** was the capital of Oklahoma for three years, until 1910, after which Oklahoma City became the capital of the state.
2. Hill 1946b; Hill 1946a; Hill 1946c; Hill and Ackiss 1943b; Hill and Ackiss 1943a.
3. Blumer 1969.
4. Hill 1946c.
5. Hill 1946b.
6. Hill 1946b; Hill and Ackiss 1943a; Hill and Ackiss 1943b.
7. In her book on Black American migration westward after Emancipation—a process that has ties to her own family history—Kendra Field (2018) describes a similar family influence and relationship to her study where some family members joined in her research travels.

Introduction

1. In this book, some identifiers for individual places (e.g., specific town establishments) and individual people (e.g., their age or occupation) have been slightly altered to protect the anonymity of the individual and community.
2. Rose 1965; Crockett 1979; Painter 1992; Turner 1999.
3. Crockett 1979; Taylor 1998; Cha-Jua 2000; Cha-Jua 2007.
4. O'Dell n.d., "All-Black Towns"; Taylor 1998.
5. Hill 1946b.
6. Black towns existed in the South as well. However, this book focuses on Oklahoma and considers the broader experience of Black towns in the West, as the town-formation process in the South differed in some ways from that in the West. See Crockett 1979, Taylor 1998 for discussion.
7. Migration to form Reconstruction-era and immediate post-Reconstruction-era Black towns occurred slightly before historians mark the beginning of the Great Migration in 1916. The conditions in the South that prompted both migrations were similar. The Great Migration, however, was also motivated by wage-labor opportunities in the industrializing North, while Black-town formation was motivated by freer and available conditions of place along with opportunities for self-employment.
8. Another way that Native Americans were involved in Black-town settlement concerns the nineteenth-century "land rush" process in the western part of what is now Oklahoma. In 1893, when the federal government opened up for settlement lands belonging to American Indians in the area known as Oklahoma Territory, Black

Americans coming from the South seized lands alongside Whites to begin forming Black towns. For more on this, see Littlefield and Underhill 1973.

9. Grinde and Taylor 1984.

10. Hamilton 1991.

11. Crockett 1979; Hill 1946a; Hill 1946c; Littlefield and Underhill 1973; Taylor 2006.

12. Research on African diasporic encounters, especially among African Americans and Afro-Caribbeans and Afro-Europeans, has shown that, in general, the relations are mixed, with discord and unity (see, for example, Thomas 2004; J. N. Brown 2005; Neptune 2007; B. C. Williams 2018). For Freedmen and African Americans in the context of Black-town life, Grinde and Taylor (1984) explain that the divisions especially concerned Freedmen's belief that African Americans were deferential to Whites; Grinde and Taylor also point out that the racial hostility that impacted both groups was a point of convergence.

13. Grinde and Taylor 1984.

14. Hill 1946a; Hill 1946b.

15. Littlefield and Underhill 1973; Painter 1992.

16. Crockett 1979; Littlefield and Underhill 1973; Painter 1992.

17. Crockett 1979; Taylor 1998; Hamilton 1977.

18. Crockett 1979; Littlefield and Underhill 1973.

19. Painter 1992.

20. Littlefield and Underhill 1973.

21. Historians studying Black towns have typically cited thirty as the number of towns that existed in Oklahoma. However, in the early 2000s the Oklahoma Historical Society updated its count to fifty. The change in the figure is an acknowledgment of towns that were not formally incorporated but were informally recognized by a populace. O'Dell 2004; O'Dell n.d., "All-Black Towns"; Taylor 1998.

22. Washington 1908; Woodson 1930; Crockett 1979; Bittle and Geis 1957; Littlefield and Underhill 1973; Taylor 1998; see also Stuckey 2009.

23. Washington 1908; Woodson 1930; Crockett 1979; Franklin 1982; O'Dell, n.d., "All-Black Towns; O'Dell 2004; Taylor 1998; Johnson 2002; Stuckey 2018.

24. Bittle and Geis 1957; Carney 1991; Crockett 1979.

25. Crockett 1979; Hill 1946b.

26. Bittle and Geis 1957; Crockett 1979; Hill 1946b; Taylor 1998.

27. O'Dell 2004; Crockett 1979.

28. Bittle and Geis 1957; Carney 1991; Crockett 1979; O'Dell, n.d., "All-Black Towns"; O'Dell 2004.

29. Bittle and Geis 1957; Crockett 1979; Franklin 1982; Hamilton 1977; Stuckey 2009; Taylor 1998; Littlefield and Underhill 1973.

30. There is a voluminous body of literature on Blacks and the ailing inner city. The 1965 report by former senator Daniel Moynihan (U.S. Department of Labor, Office of Planning and Research 1965) is often referenced as defining urban Black communities as pathological. Since then, a number of sociological and policy studies have analyzed conditions of Black communities that are of concern, or have proposed policies to address those conditions. While the studies and reports are too numerous to cite, especial key sources include the 1968 Kerner Report on unrest and economic condi-

tions in urban areas (National Advisory Commission on Civil Disorders 1968); works by sociologist William Julius Wilson (1978, 1987) on labor-market demands and conditions of Black urban life; and Douglass Massey and Nancy Denton (1993) on the impact of racial segregation on Black urban communities.

31. Patillo-McCoy 1999; Feagin and Sikes 1995.

32. Lacy 2007.

33. Hunter and Robinson 2018.

34. Hill 1946a; Hill 1946b.

35. McKittrick 2011.

36. Massey 1994.

37. Feld and Basso 1996, "Introduction," 1–11.

38. As mentioned, McKittrick pulls from geographer Doreen Massey (1994), who wrote of a "global sense of place," underscoring how places are enmeshed in multiple, vast, and uneven networks and social relations where power dynamics influence how different people move through place. It is the idea of a quality or significant feature of place made or informed by structural influences in which there is unevenness of mobility—due to what Massey calls a "power geometry"—that is especially resonant between a global sense of place and a Black sense of place. However, the global sense of place is about locality within a range of global economic and social flows, while a Black sense of place is about locality within spatial inequalities specific to race. A global sense of place is itself comprised of spatial inequalities (hence the social unevenness of mobility), but the sites significant in shaping a Black sense of place are specific to Black experiences. (See Cresswell 2004 for further discussion of Massey's argument.)

39. McKittrick 2011, 948.

40. McKittrick 2011, 949.

41. McKittrick and Woods 2007.

42. Robinson 1983; Kelley 2002.

43. Roberts 2015, 5; Bledsoe 2017.

44. Roberts 2015, 5.

45. Besson 2002; Mintz 1958; Slocum 2017.

46. Strain 2004; Minchin 2005; Fergus 2010; Purifoy 2018b.

47. McKittrick 2011.

48. Hunter and Robinson 2018, 88.

49. Lipsitz 2007. For examples, see also Gilmore 2007; Woods 1998.

50. Ralph 2014; Patillo-McCoy 1999; Gregory 1998.

51. Gupta and Ferguson 1997; Rodman 1992; Massey 1994.

52. Gupta and Ferguson 1997; Low 2016.

53. McKittrick 2011, 250.

54. Woods 1998; Eaves 2017.

55. McKittrick 2011; Woods 1998; Eaves 2017.

56. Hunter and Robinson 2018, 88.

57. Morrison 1998.

58. Gregory 1998.

59. Ralph 2014.

60. Polanco 2014.

61. Robinson 2004.

62. Lipsitz 2011; Lipsitz 2018.

63. McKittrick 2011, 950.

64. U.S. Census Bureau 2000; U.S. Census Bureau 2010.

65. U.S. Census Bureau 2010.

66. Raymond 2012; Waits Jr., n.d.

67. U.S. Census Bureau 2010.

68. U.S. Census Bureau 2010; U.S. Census Bureau 2000.

69. Woods 2007.

70. Stack 1996.

71. Davidson 1996; Dudley 2000; Sherman 2009.

72. The literature on neoliberal economies is voluminous. Especially influential in anthropology have been David Harvey's (2005, 1989) texts *A Brief History of Neoliberalism* and *The Condition of Post Modernity: An Enquiry into the Origins of Cultural Change.* For a review of anthropological sources on neoliberalism, see Ganti 2014.

73. Housing Assistance Council 2005.

74. Sturm 2014.

75. U.S. Census Bureau 2010.

76. U.S. Census Bureau 2010.

77. Drake and Clayton 1945; Gregory 1998; Patillo-McCoy 1999; Vargas 2006; Ralph 2014.

Chapter One

1. Richards 2005; Pierre 2012; Holsey 2017.

2. Richards 2005, 632.

3. Holsey 2017, 481.

4. For discussions of this trend, and some specific examples, see Drake 1987; Drake and Cayton 1945; Foster 1997; Scott 2004.

5. Works especially influential here include Crockett 1979; Hamilton 1977; Franklin 1982; Taylor 2006; Stuckey 2009.

6. Michel-Rolph Trouillot (1997) discusses how narratives of history in Haiti are partial and effacing, just as the Oklahoma History Center narrative of Black-town history, through their Black-town signs, mute the terror that Black-town residents recount in more detail. Discussing narratives of communities labeled "historically black," Mieka Polanco (2014) also demonstrates that there are divergent and sometimes competing histories of place told by community members who differ by race and other social positions.

7. Crockett 1979; Hill 1946b. In addition to scholarly sources that connect Black-town formation to Booker T. Washington's work, some Black towns, especially in the Southeast, reference their communities' historic ties to Washington or credit Washington with the Black-town movement in their promotional material and online town histories. Examples of this include Mound Bayou, Mississippi, and Eatonville, Florida.

8. Hill 1946b.

9. Washington 1908.

10. Crockett (1979) also looks critically at the towns, with much emphasis on the struggles and pitfalls they experienced in their attempts to keep their communities afloat. While his book is part of the "historical success" narrative because it outlines the major town developments and strides in politics, economics, and social life, it also discusses at length the towns' complications. Ultimately, the book concludes with Black towns' decline, in a final chapter on "Frustration and Failure," which is also in keeping with the narrative that locates Black-town success before 1940. Yet Crockett's book is still leveraged today for popular writings that discuss Black towns' historic success, contrasted with their present condition as one of struggle to survive.

11. Crockett 1979. Crockett understands Oklahoma as based geographically outside of the South. However, Oklahoma elides easy geographic placement. In fact, before the end of the first decade of the twentieth century, involuntary and voluntary migrations from the Southeast populated and shaped what would become Oklahoma, giving the eventual state significant ties to and influence from what is considered the indisputable South. But most often, and for a mix of geographic and cultural reasons, Oklahoma is viewed as being part of the Southwest, the Midwest, or just the West.

12. Eaton 2015; Hardzinski 2015; Taylor 2012; O'Dell 2004.

13. O'Dell n.d., "Boley."

14. Littlefield and Underhill 1973.

15. Washington 1908.

16. Hill 1946b, 46.

17. People claiming German ancestry represented one-eighth of the Oklahoma population at the beginning of the twenty-first century (Robinson 2004). German migration to Oklahoma occurred between the end of the nineteenth and beginning of the twentieth century, with Germans never representing more than 3 percent of the state's population (Rohrs 1980).

18. Walker 1996.

19. Anderson 1988.

20. Cross 2015.

21. Humphrey 1978.

22. Hoffschwelle 2006.

23. O'Dell n.d., "Lima."

24. Adichie 2009.

Chapter Two

1. Oklahoma Historical Society n.d.

2. Boyd 2008, 70. Mieka Polanco (2014) also argues that the designation "historically significant" is constructed and has variable meaning based on the interests and agendas of who is narrating the history of Black places. It is also contested.

3. Holsey 2008; Pierre 2012; Bruner 2004.

4. Thomas 2009.

5. Ashworth 1994; Boyd 2008.

6. Thomas 2009, 752–53.

7. Escobar 2001; Massey 2005; Low 2016.

8. Low 2016; Massey 2007.

9. Jackson 2000.

10. Boyd 2008.

11. I focus on Allen's narrative due to his prominent positioning in one of the most popular Black-town tours. As there are multiple tours of Black towns, he is not the only tour narrator, and, importantly, his account of Black-town history is not in line with other accounts tourists can hear, even on tours sponsored by the same company that used Allen as a narrator. Many tour narratives are in line with what I would call "conventional" historians' accounts, highlighting the boom and bust periods of Black towns, the institutional strength during the boom period, and the national and Oklahoma-specific political, social, environmental, and economic dynamics that led to a decline in the Black-town population starting around the 1920s. This is the Black-town-history story discussed in the book's introduction and chapter 1. I highlight Allen's account because of tour sponsors' and tourists' high regard for his narrative and insights, even though at least one other tour narrator cautioned me against placing too much stock in Allen's analysis.

12. Grinde and Taylor 1984.

13. Van Sertima, 1976.

14. Van Sertima based his argument largely on the phenotype shown on stone representations of the Olmecs from ancient Mexico. Van Sertima contended that the presence of African features on the Olmec heads provided evidence of contact with Africans.

15. DeLoria 1995.

16. In the 1988 "A Declaration of First Nations," Canadian indigenous groups outline their belief that their origins in North America was due to the Creator.

17. Chang 2002; Chang 2006; Chang 2010; McAuley 1998.

18. Chang 2002, 142.

19. William McAuley (1998) found the distinction between Native and non-Native Blacks in the Oklahoma Black towns where he researched elders' connection to place in the communities. A decade later, I did not encounter this distinction during my own research.

20. Chang 2006.

21. National Museum of African American History and Culture n.d., *Power of Place*.

22. Holsey 2008; Pierre 2012; Ebron 1999; Richards 2005.

23. U.S. Census Bureau 2011; Community Service Council 2019.

24. Community Service Council 2019.

25. Community Service Council 2019.

26. H. Johnson 1998.

27. H. Johnson 1998; Oklahoma Commission 2001.

28. Chang 2006; Sturm 2002. Federal assignments of American Indians to the Dawes Rolls, as they are called, were based on a person's degree of "Indian blood." Thus, tribal members were divided according to their blood quantum, measured in

quarters. Freedmen, although added to the rolls, were set apart as having zero degree of Indian blood but being members based on prior enslavement. In recent times this division has been the source of heated debate and protracted lawsuits. In the early 2000s, the Cherokee Nation decided to exclude tribal members who, based on the Dawes Rolls, could not prove that they contained at least one-quarter degree of Indian blood. For a discussion of blood quantum requirements in the process of defining American Indian status, see especially Meyer (1999) and also Garroutte (2001). For anthropological discussions of the process in specific tribes of Oklahoma, see Dennison (2012), Lambert (2009), and Sturm (2002).

29. Chang 2006.

30. Sturm 2002.

31. Sturm 2002.

32. Oklahoma Historical Society 1991.

33. Hanna and Culpepper 1997.

34. Honey Springs National Battlefield and Washita Battlefield National Historic Site Act of 1994.

35. The First Kansas Colored Infantry was made up of former and freed slaves who were recruited by a Kansas senator to fight in the Civil War. They were the first African American combat unit (see Spurgeon 2014) and fought in battles across the West, in Kansas, Missouri, Arkansas, and Indian Territory (see also National Park Service n.d.).

36. "Fort Gibson Historic Site and Interpretive Center" n.d.

37. LeRoi H. Fischer, "Honey Springs Battlefield National Park: The Battle of Honey Springs, July 17, 1863," [n.p.: monograph January 1969], quoted in Oklahoma Historical Society 1991, 3.

38. Oklahoma Historical Society 1991.

39. Trouillot 1990.

Chapter Three

1. U.S. Census Bureau 2012. Among Black-town officials, there is some disagreement with census data on Black-town racial demographics, particularly those data that mark some towns as having a population over a thousand and a sizeable White population. Census data count inmates in the prisons located in some Black towns, skewing the numbers on who owns or rents a home dwelling and regularly resides in the towns. No Black-town government official whom I spoke with considered any Black town to have a population greater than six hundred.

2. Creed and Ching 1997; Wood 2007.

3. U.S. Department of Labor, Office of Policy Planning and Research 1965.

4. Boyd 2008; Checker 2005; Gregory 1998; Patillo-McCoy 1999.

5. Boyd 2008; Gregory 1998.

6. Ralph 2014.

7. Perez 2004; Prince 2014; Lees, Slater, and Wyly 2008. While there are many social-science studies of gentrification showing the deleterious impacts, Lance Freeman's (2006) study stands out for its argument that gentrification not only improves

communities (especially Black American and Latino communities) but is welcomed by residents.

8. Lees, Slater, and Wyly 2008; Perez 2004; Prince 2014.

9. Thiede and Slack 2017.

10. Hill 1946b, 46.

11. Hill 1946b.

12. The literature has been silent on gender and Black towns; however, from the discussions of the Black-town past there is a common image of male leadership in Black-town economies and formal governance as well as state politics (Stuckey 2009). It is thus striking that, today, women are active in Black-town business and government. In Promise and Wrightsville, the most visible and sustained businesses (one per town) are owned and run by women. In Newtown, a woman runs one of the community's major establishments, while a husband-wife team runs another business. Informal economic activities are also where we find women's presence. Moreover, women are frequently present as town mayors or town council members. During my research, a majority of the towns had a female mayor at some point. This apparent gender shift, I suggest, is likely due in part to changing gender roles for women in the country but also to the frequency of women who return to Black towns after working until retirement age in major U.S. cities. Many return to care for elderly family members or to reconnect with home, and then they become actively involved in town events and governance.

13. Class distinctions in Black towns are noted in the literature. Hill (1946b) initially argued that there was a loose social hierarchy in Black towns such that mobility was possible among the different strata. However, he also referenced sharp class distinctions in opinions about whether engagement with Whites is acceptable (Hill 1946b) or whether wealthier residents were more open to change than poorer residents (Hill and Ackiss 1943a). Other scholars have discussed palpable divisions and hierarchies based on heritage/ancestry (McAuley 1998) and color (Hill 1946b) into the late nineteenth century. Celia's mention of a "crabs-in-a-barrel" issue—in which residents with more income are not willing to help out and support those with less—does not come up in the literature but is supported by other interviewees in my study, raising questions about how class divisions interact with principles about racial solidarity, as was the question that Hill (1946b) explored in depth.

14. Nelson, Oberg, and Nelson 2010; Darling 2005; Hines 2010.

15. Nelson, Oberg, and Nelson 2010; Housing Assistance Council 2005.

16. Housing Assistance Council 2005.

17. Hill 1946b.

18. Hill 1946b, 131.

19. For discussion of counterurbanization and gentrification as related phenomena, see especially Phillips 2010.

20. U.S. Census Bureau 2000; U.S. Census Bureau 2010. As mentioned, among Black-town residents there is disbelief in some of the census data on Black towns, including the number of Whites who are counted as resident in the communities. McAuley (1998) notes concerns with census data and, concurring with my research,

estimates that more than 95 percent of all remaining Black towns contain residents who identify as "Black."

21. Drake and Clayton 1945.

22. Hill 1946b.

23. Gilmore 2007.

24. Alexander 2010.

25. King, Mauer, and Huling 2003.

26. Eason 2010; Eason 2017.

27. Eason 2010; Eason 2017.

28. Sentencing Project 2004; Oklahoma Department of Corrections 2002.

29. Simmons 2013.

30. Jaworski 2013; Beale 1996; Beale 1993; King, Mauer, and Huling 2003.

31. Casteel 1986a; Casteel 1986b.

32. This economic impact in Oklahoma's Black towns reflects a broader national trend. Since the 1980s, scant economic and employment benefits have accrued to rural "prison towns" (King, Mauer, and Huling 2003; Hooks et al. 2004; Beale 1996; Gilmore 2007). Despite how prisons have been promoted and the hopes of rural residents who lobby for prisons to arrive in their towns, a low percentage of jobs goes to residents (Besser and Hanson 2004).

33. Donovan 1983.

34. Then-mayor of **Taft** Leila Foley Davis reportedly said, "I feel like part of the reason [that the center is being closed] is because **Taft** is a Black community" (Brawley 1986). Additionally, Oklahoma's senator E. Melvin Porter, who filed a lawsuit against prisons coming to **Taft**, was quoted in the *Daily Oklahoman* as saying, "I as a Black citizen, resent [the building of prisons in **Boley**]. . . . I don't think it would have occurred in any other state" (Donovan 1983).

35. Beesley 2009.

36. Melissa Schrift (2004) argues that prison rodeos, which also take place in Texas and Louisiana, are "recreational tourism," spectacles that further subjugate incarcerated individuals by making them objects of attraction. In contrast, *Sweethearts of the Prison Rodeo* profiles the rodeo as a motivational event that gives inmates something to look forward to. Schrift would likely contend that the film contributes to the spectacle of the event.

Chapter Four

1. Stack 1996.

2. Frey 2004; Frey 2015.

3. Frey 2004.

4. Long and Moore 2012; Amit 2012.

5. The **Rentiesville** Dusk 'til Dawn Blues Festival has existed since 2001. It was begun by blues musician DC Minner, who was from **Rentiesville** and ran a blues club that still operates today. Minner passed away in 2008. His wife, Selby Minner, now hosts the festival. Among Black towns, the festival rivals the **Boley** Rodeo in terms of the number of participants.

6. Raymond 2012.

7. Stuckey 2018.

8. Stuckey 2018.

9. Stuckey 2018.

10. According to Marvin Kroeker (n.d.), the Mennonite congregation came to **Boley** in the 1970s, having migrated from Mexico. The community exists in a separate location of the town, but members are seen around town at the post office and other public facilities.

11. Sandoval 2013.

12. National Museum of African American History and Culture n.d., "Lowriders."

13. Wilkins 2016.

14. Sandoval 2013, 180.

15. Thomas 2004.

16. Hill 1946c.

17. Regis 1999; Stillman and Villmoare 2010.

18. Regis 1999.

19. Miller-Cribbs 2004.

20. McCoy 2011; Miller-Cribbs 2004.

21. Hill 1946a.

22. Johnson 1941.

23. Hill 1946a, 27.

24. Amit 2018.

Chapter Five

1. Rose 1965.

2. Cha-Jua 2000.

3. Wiese 1993.

4. Nieves 2008.

5. Lipsitz 2007.

Epilogue

1. Purifoy 2018a.

2. Sanchez 2017.

3. Elswick 2017.

4. "Quake Rattles the Town of Boley," 2013.

5. Raymond 2012.

6. Barber 2017.

7. Nine reels of silent, black-and-white film from the collection of Reverend Solomon Sir Jones are now available online at the National Museum of African American History and Culture (NMAAHC), depicting everyday Black middle-class life in 1920s urban and small-town Oklahoma. Other organizations also have some of the footage online. For an example from NMAAHC, see https://nmaahc.si.edu/object/nmaahc_2011.79.1.1abc (retrieved August 5, 2019).

8. U.S. Census Bureau, 2006–2010, American Community Survey; U.S. Census Bureau, 2013–2017, American Community Survey, generated by American Factfinder, December 29, 2018.

9. Polanco 2014.

10. Gibson 2018.

11. Feldhousen-Giles 2008.

12. K. Brown 2018; Ulrich-Schad and Duncan 2018. The authors find that in the rural, Black, and high-poverty areas such as the southern Black Belt and Mississippi Delta, voting was more split between Democratic and Republican than in majority-White, poor, rural areas.

13. Tieken 2017.

Glossary of Place Names

Boley a Black town

Carson a pseudonym for an actual historically White town near Wrightsville

Fort Coffee unofficially regarded as a Black town

Freeland a pseudonym for an actual Black town

Green Valley a pseudonym for an actual Black town

Guthrie a small city, former capital of Oklahoma

Jewel a pseudonym for an actual unincorporated Black town near Freeland

Kidder a pseudonym for an actual satellite community of Newtown

King's Prairie a pseudonym for an actual unincorporated Black town near Freeland

Langston a Black town

Lima a Black town

Muskogee a small city in Oklahoma

Newtown a pseudonym for an actual Black town

Oklahoma City one of the two largest cities in Oklahoma and capital of the state

Okmulgee a small city in Oklahoma

Pineway a pseudonym for an actual Black town near Promise

Promise a pseudonym for an actual Black town

Redbird a Black town

Rentiesville a Black town

Summit a Black town

Taft a Black town

Tatums a Black Town

Tullahassee a Black Town

Tulsa one of the two largest cities in Oklahoma

Wrightsville a pseudonym for an actual Black town

Bibliography

Adichie, Chimimanda Ngozi. 2009. "The Danger of a Single Story." TED video, 18:43. https://www.ted.com/talks/chimamanda_adichie_the_danger_of_a _single_story?language=en.

Alexander, Michelle. 2010. *The New Jim Crow: Mass Incarceration in the Age of Colorblindness*. New York: New Press.

Amit, Vered. 2018. *Thinking through Sociality: An Anthropological Interrogation of Key Concepts*. Brooklyn: Berghahn Books.

Anderson, James D. 1988. *The Education of Blacks in the South, 1860–1935*. Chapel Hill: University of North Carolina Press.

Ashworth, G. J. 1994. "From History to Heritage — From Heritage to Identity: In Search of Concepts and Models." In *Building a New Heritage! Tourism, Culture and Identity in the New Europe*, edited by G. J. Ashworth and P. J. Lanham, 13–30. London: Routledge.

Assembly of First Nations. 1988. "A Declaration of First Nations." https://www.afn .ca/about-afn/declaration-of-first-nations/.

Barber, Kari, dir. 2017. *Struggle and Hope*. Independent Television Service. 65 min.

Beale, Calvin. 1993. "Prisons, Population and Jobs in Nonmetro America." *Rural Development Perspectives* 8 (3): 16–19.

———. 1996. "Rural Prisons: An Update." *Rural Development Perspectives* 11 (2): 25–27.

Beesley, Bradley, dir. 2009. *Sweethearts of the Prison Rodeo*. HBO Documentary Films and Fieldguide Media. DVD release 2010.

Besser, Terry L., and Margaret M. Hanson. 2004. "The Development of Last Resort: The Impact of New State Prisons on Small Town Economies in the United States." *Journal of the Community Development Society* 35 (2): 1–16.

Besson, Jean. 2002. *Martha Brae's Two Histories: European Expansion and Caribbean Culture-Building in Jamaica*. Chapel Hill: University of North Carolina Press.

Bittle, William, and Gilbert Geis. 1957. "Racial Self-Fulfillment and the Rise of an All-Negro Community in Oklahoma." *The Phylon Quarterly* 18 (3): 247–60.

Bledsoe, Adam. 2017. "Marronage as a Past and Present Geography in the Americas." *Southeastern Geographer* 57 (1): 30–50.

Blumer, Herbert. 1969. *Symbolic Interactionism: Perspectives and Method*. Englewood Cliffs, NJ: Prentiss Hall.

Bonilla Silva, Eduardo. 2003. *Racism without Racists: Color-Blind Racism and the Persistence of Racial Inequality in America*. Lanham, MD: Rowman and Littlefield.

Boyd, Michelle. 2008. *Jim Crow Nostalgia: Reconstructing Race in Bronzeville*. Minneapolis: University of Minnesota Press.

Brawley, Chris. 1986. "Closing Taft Will Free Some Delinquents." *Daily Oklahoman* (Oklahoma City). March 9.

Brown, Jacquelyn Nassy. 2005. *Dropping Anchor, Setting Sail: Geographies of Race in Black Liverpool*. Princeton, NJ: Princeton University Press.

Brown, Karida. 2018. *Gone Home: Race and Roots through Appalachia*. Chapel Hill: University of North Carolina Press.

Bruner, Edward. 2004. *Culture on Tour: Ethnographies of Travel*. Chicago: University of Chicago Press.

Carney, George. 1991. "Historic Resources of Oklahoma's All-Black Towns." *Chronicles of Oklahoma* 62 (2): 116–33.

Casteel, Chris. 1986a. "$1 Million Allotted to Expand Prison: Panel Funds 150 More Beds at Taft." *Daily Oklahoman* (Oklahoma City). June 6.

———. 1986b. "House OK's Taft Center for Training of Guards." *Daily Oklahoman* (Oklahoma City). May 13.

Cha-Jua, Sundiata. 2000. *America's First Black Town, Brooklyn, Illinois, 1830–1915*. Urbana: University of Illinois Press.

———. 2007. "African Americans in Suburbs and African American Towns." In *Encyclopedia of American Urban History*. edited by David Goldstein, 13–18. Thousand Oaks: Sage Publications.

Chang, David A. 2006. "Where Will the Nation Be at Home? Race, Nationalisms and Emigration Movements in the Creek Nation." In *Crossing Waters, Crossing Worlds: The African Diaspora in Indian Country*, edited by Tiya Miles and Sharon P. Holland, 100–120. Durham, NC: Duke University Press.

———. 2010. *The Color of the Land: Race, Nation, and the Politics of Landownership in Oklahoma, 1832–1929*. Chapel Hill: University of North Carolina Press.

Chang, David A. Y. O. 2002. "From Indian Territory to White Man's Country: Race, Nation, and the Politics of Land Ownership." PhD diss., University of Wisconsin–Madison.

Checker, Melissa. 2005. *Polluted Promises: Environmental Racism and the Search for Justice in a Southern Town*. New York: NYU Press.

Clarke, Kamari. 2006. "Mapping Transnationality: Roots Tourism and the Institutionalization of Ethnic Heritage." In *Globalization and Race: Transformations in the Cultural Production of Blackness*, edited by M. Kamari Clarke and Deborah Thomas, 133–53. Durham, NC: Duke University Press.

Community Service Council. 2011. "Population Trends: Tulsa County, Tulsa and North Tulsa 2000 to 2010." Unpublished file prepared by the Community Service Council, with support from the Metropolitan Human Services Commission. Tulsa, OK.

———. 2019. "North Tulsa Trends, 1960–2010 by Race." Unpublished file prepared by the Community Service Council, with support from the Metropolitan Human Services Commission. Tulsa, OK.

Creed, Gerald, and Barbara Ching. 1997. "Recognizing Rusticity: Identity and the Power of Place." In *Knowing Your Place*, edited by Barbara Ching and Gerald Creed, 1–38. New York: Routledge.

Cresswell, Tim. 2004. *Place: A Short Introduction*. Malden, MA: Blackwell.

Crockett, Norman. 1979. *The Black Towns*. Lawrence: Regents Press of Kansas.

Cross, Phil. 2015. "Considering Consolidation: Losing a School." Oklahoma City Fox 25. October 28. https://okcfox.com/news/fox-25-investigates/considering -consolidation-losing-a-school.

Darling, Eliza. 2005. "The City in the Country: Wilderness Gentrification and the Rent Gap." *Environment and Planning A* 37 (6): 1015–32.

Davidson, Osha Gray. 1996. *Broken Heartland: The Rise of America's Rural Ghetto.* Iowa City: University of Iowa Press.

Davis, Angela Y. 2003. *Are Prisons Obsolete?* New York: Seven Stories Press.

DeLoria, Vine. 1995. *Red Earth, White Lies: Native Americans and the Myth of Scientific Fact.* New York: Scribner.

Dennison, Jean. 2012. *Colonial Entanglement: Constituting a Twenty-First-Century Osage Nation.* Chapel Hill: University of North Carolina Press.

Donovan, Kevin. 1983. "Judge Rules Legislative Actions Squelch Suit over Boley School Transfer." *Daily Oklahoman* (Oklahoma City). July 2.

Drake, St. Clair. 1987. *Black Folk Here and There.* Los Angeles: Center for Afro-American Studies, University of California.

Drake, St. Clair, and Horace Cayton. 1945. *Black Metropolis: A Study of Negro Life in a Northern City.* New York: Harcourt, Brace and Company.

Dudley, Katherine. 2000. *Debt and Dispossession: Farm Loss in America's Heartland.* Chicago: University of Chicago press.

Eason, John. 2010. "Mapping Prison Proliferation: Region, Rurality, Race, and Disadvantage in Prison Placement." *Social Science Research* 39: 1015–28.

Eason, John M. 2017. *Big House on the Prairie: Rise of the Rural Ghetto and Prison Proliferation.* Chicago: University of Chicago Press.

Eaton, Kristi. 2015. "Once Forgotten, Oklahoma's Historic All-Black Towns Find Renewed Interest." Aljazeera America. August 4. http://america.aljazeera.com /articles/2015/8/4/once-forgotten-oklahomas-historic-all-Black-towns-find -renewed-interest.html.

Eaves, LaToya. 2017. "Black Geographic Possibilities: On a Queer Black South." *Southeastern Geographer* 57 (1): 80–95.

Ebron, Paulla. 2000. "Tourists as Pilgrims: Commercial Fashioning of Transatlantic Politics." *American Ethnologist* 26 (4): 910–32.

Elswick, Mike. 2017. "Water Hookup Attempts Come Up Dry." Muskogee Phoenix. June 18. https://www.muskogeephoenix.com/news/water-hookup-attempts -come-up dry/article_31b3475e-9f12-5ba3-82f3-664582316315.html.

Escobar, Arturo. 2001. "Culture Sits in Places: Reflections on Globalism and Subaltern Strategies of Localization." *Political Geography* 20: 139–74.

Feagin, Joseph, and Melvin P. Sikes. 1995. *Living with Racism: The Black Middle Class Experience.* New York: Beacon Press.

Feld, Steven, and Keith Basso, eds. 1996. *Senses of Place.* Santa Fe, NM: School for Advanced Research.

Feldhousen-Giles, Kristy. 2008. "To Prove Who You Are: Freedmen Identities in Oklahoma." PhD diss., University of Oklahoma, Norman.

Fergus, Devin. 2010. "Black Power, Soft Power: Floyd McKissick, Soul City, and the Death of Moderate Black Republicanism." *Journal of Policy History* 22 (2): 148–92.

Field, Kendra Taira. 2018. *Growing Up with the Country: Family, Race, and Nation after the Civil War*. New Haven, CT: Yale University Press.

"Fort Gibson Historic Site and Interpretive Center." n.d. Travel OK website. Accessed March 30, 2019. https://www.travelok.com/listings/view.profile /id.2825.

Foster, Kevin Michael. 1997. "Vindicationist Politics: A Foundation and Point of Departure for an African Diaspora Studies Paradigm." *Transforming Anthropology* 6 (1/2): 2–9.

Franklin, Jimmie Lewis. 1982. *Journey toward Hope: A History of Blacks in Oklahoma*. Norman: University of Oklahoma Press.

Freeman, Lance. 2006. *There Goes the 'Hood: Views of Gentrification from the Ground Up*. Philadelphia: Temple University Press.

Frey, William H. 2004. *The New Great Migration: Black Americans' Return to the South, 1965–2000*. Living Cities Census Series. Washington, DC: Brookings Institution Press.

———. 2015. *Diversity Explosion: How New Racial Demographics Are Remaking America*. Washington, DC: Brookings Institution Press.

Garroutte, Eva Marie. 2001. "The Racial Formation of American Indians: Negotiating Legitimate Identities within Tribal and Federal Law." *American Indian Quarterly* 25 (2): 224–39.

Gibson, Tiffany. 2018. "MAP: Comparing 2016, 2012 Presidential Precinct-Level Results in Oklahoma." November 10. https://newsok.com/article/5525907 /map-comparing-2016-2012-presidential-precinct-level-results-in-oklahoma.

Gilmore, Ruth Wilson. 2007. *Golden Gulag: Surplus, Crisis and Opposition in Globalizing California*. Berkeley: University of California Press.

Gray, Linda. 1988–89. "Taft: Town on the Black Frontier." *Chronicles of Oklahoma* 66 (4): 430–47.

Gregory, Stephen. 1998. *Black Corona: Race and the Politics of Place in an Urban Community*. Princeton, NJ: Princeton University Press.

Grinde, Donald A., Jr., and Quintard Taylor. 1984. "Red vs. Black: Conflict and Accommodation in the Post–Civil War Indian Territory, 1865–1907." *American Indian Quarterly* 8 (3): 211–29.

Gupta, Akhil, and James Ferguson. 1997. "Culture, Power, Place: Ethnography at the End of an Era." In *Culture, Power, Place: Explorations in Critical Anthropology*, edited by Akhil Gupta and James Ferguson, 1–32. Durham, NC: Duke University Press.

Hamilton, Kenneth. 1991. *Black Towns and Profit: Promotion and Development in the Trans-Appalachian West, 1877–1915*. Urbana: University of Illinois Press.

Hanna, Karen, and R. Brian Culpepper. 1997. *Honey Springs Battlefield Park: Master Plan Report*. Prepared for Battlefield Protection Program and Oklahoma Historical Society, Center for Advanced Spatial Technologies, University of Arkansas.

Hardzinski, Brian. 2015. "Why Indian Territory's All-Black Towns Prospered While Most of Oklahoma Territory's Faded Away." KGOU. August 3. http://www.kgou .org/post/why-indian-territorys-all-black-towns-prospered-while-most -oklahoma-territorys-faded-away.

Harvey, David. 1989. *The Condition of Postmodernity: An Enquiry into the Origins of Cultural Change*. Cambridge, MA: Blackwell.

———. 2005. *A Brief History of Neoliberalism*. New York: Oxford University Press.

Hill, Mozell. 1946a. "The All-Negro Communities of Oklahoma: The Natural History of a Social Movement," Part I. *Journal of Negro History* 31 (3): 254–68.

———. 1946b. "The All-Negro Society in Oklahoma." PhD diss., University of Chicago.

———. 1946c. "A Comparative Analysis of the Social Organization of the All-Negro Society in Oklahoma." *Social Forces* 25 (1): 70–77.

Hill, Mozell C., and Thelma D. Ackiss. 1943a. *Culture of a Contemporary All-Negro Community*. Langston, OK: Langston University.

———. 1943b. "Social Classes: A Frame of Reference for the Study of Negro Society." *Social Forces* 22 (1): 92–98.

Hines, J. Dwight. 2010. "Rural Gentrification as Permanent Tourism: The Creation of the 'New' West Archipelago as Postindustrial Cultural Space." *Environment and Planning D: Society and Space* 28 (3): 509–25.

Hoffschwelle, Mary. 2006. *The Rosenwald Schools of the American South*. Gainesville: University Press of Florida.

Holsey, Bayo. 2008. *Routes of Remembrance: Refashioning the Slave Trade in Ghana*. Chicago: University of Chicago Press.

———. 2017. "Slavery Tourism: Representing a Difficult History in Ghana." In *The Oxford Handbook of Public History*, edited by Paula Hamilton and James B. Gardner, 479–71.

Honey Springs National Battlefield and Washita Battlefield National Historic Site Act of 1994. H.R. 4821. 103rd Cong., 2nd session.

Hooks, Gregory, Clayton Mosher, Thomas Rotolo, and Linda Lobao. 2004. "The Prison Industry: Carceral Expansion and Employment in U.S. Counties, 1969–1994." *Social Science Quarterly* 85 (1): 37–57.

Housing Assistance Council. 2005. *They Paved Paradise . . . Gentrification in Rural Communities*. Washington, DC.

Humphrey, Charles A. 1978. "Educational and Social Needs in Small All-Black Towns." *Journal of Negro Education* 47 (3): 244–55.

Hunter, Marcus Anthony, and Zandria Robinson. 2018. *Chocolate Cities: The Black Map of American Life*. Berkeley: University of California Press.

Jackson, John L. 2000. *Harlemworld: Doing Race and Class in Contemporary Black America*. Chicago: University of Chicago Press.

Jaworski, Darren. 2013. "Interactive: Oklahoma's Prison System Is at Nearly Full Capacity." Oklahoma Watch. July 27, 2013. http://oklahomawatch.org/2013/07/27/oklahomas-correctional-facilities/.

Johnson, Charles. 1941. *Growing Up in the Black Belt: Negro Youth in the Rural South*. Washington, DC: American Youth Council on Education.

Johnson, Hannibal. 2002. *Acres of Aspiration: The All-Black Towns of Oklahoma*. Austin: Eakin Press.

Kelley, Robin D. G. 2002. *Freedom Dreams: The Black Radical Imagination*. New York: Beacon Press.

King, Ryan S., Marc Mauer, and Tracy Huling. 2003. *Big Prisons, Small Towns: Prison Economics in Rural America*. Washington, DC: The Sentencing Project.

Kroeker, Marvin. n.d. "Mennonites." *Encyclopedia of Oklahoma History and Culture*. Accessed April 17, 2018. https://www.okhistory.org/publications/enc.php?entry=ME012.

Lacy, Karyn. 2007. *Blue Chip Black: Race, Class and Status in the New Black Middle Class*. Berkeley: University of California Press.

Lambert, Valerie. 2009. *Choctaw Nation: A Story of American Indian Resurgence*. Lincoln: University of Nebraska Press.

Lees, Loretta, Tom Slater, and Elvin Wyly. 2008. *Gentrification*. New York: Routledge.

Lipsitz, George. 2007. "The Racialization of Space and the Spatialization of Race: Theorizing the Hidden Architecture of Landscape." *Landscape Journal* 26 (1): 10–23.

———. 2011. *How Racism Takes Place*. Philadelphia: Temple University Press.

———. 2018. "Conjuring Sacred Space in Gulf Coast Cities." *Journal of the American Academy of Religion* 86 (2): 497–525.

Littlefield, Daniel, and Lonnie Underhill. 1973. "Black Dreams and 'Free' Homes: The Oklahoma Territory, 1891–1894." *Phylon* 34 (4): 313–22.

Long, Nathan, and Henrietta Moore. 2012. "Introduction: Sociality's New Directions." In *Sociality: New Directions*, edited by Nathan Long and Henrietta Moore, 1–24. New York: Berghan Books.

Low, Setha. 2016. *Spatializing Culture: The Ethnography of Space and Place*. New York: Routledge.

Massey, Doreen. 1994. *Space, Place, and Gender*. Minneapolis: University of Minnesota Press.

———. 2005. *For Space*. London: Sage Publications.

———. 2007. *World City*. Cambridge: Polity Press.

Massey, Douglas, and Nancy Denton. 1993. *American Apartheid: Segregation and the Making of the Underclass*. Cambridge, MA: Harvard University Press.

McAuley, William. 1998. "History, Race, and Attachment to Place among Elders in the Rural All-Black Towns of Oklahoma." *Journal of Gerontology, Social Sciences* 53B: S35–S45.

McCoy, Renee. 2011. "African American Elders, Cultural Traditions, and the Family Reunion." *Generations* 35 (3): 16–21.

McKittrick, Katherine. 2011. "On Plantations, Prisons, and a Black Sense of Place." *Social and Cultural Geography* 12 (8): 947–63.

McKittrick, Katherine, and Clyde Woods. 2007. *Black Geographies and the Politics of Place*. Cambridge, MA: South End Press.

Meyer, Melissa. 1999. "American Indian Blood Quantum Requirements: Blood Is Thicker than Family." In *Over the Edge: Remapping the American West*, edited by Valerie J. Matsumoto and Blake Allmendinger, 231–49. Berkeley: University of California Press.

Miller-Cribbs, J. 2004. "African-American Family Reunions: Directions for Future Research and Practice." *African American Research Perspectives* 10 (1): 160–73.

Minchin, Timothy J. 2005. "'A Brand New Shining City': Floyd B. McKissick Sr. and the Struggle to Build Soul City, North Carolina." *North Carolina Historical Review* 82 (2): 125–55.

Mintz, Sidney. 1958. "The Historical Sociology of the Jamaican Church-Founded Free Village System." *De West-Indische Gids* 38 (1–2): 46–70.

Morrison, Toni. 1998. *Paradise*. New York: Knopf.

National Advisory Commission on Civil Disorders. 1968. *Kerner Commission Summary Report*. Washington, DC: U.S. Government Printing Office. https://www.hsdl.org/?abstract&did=35837.

National Museum of African American History and Culture. n.d. "Lowriders: Cars with Identities." Accessed June 15, 2018. https://nmaahc.si.edu/explore/manylenses/lowriders.

———. n.d. *Power of Place*. Permanent Exhibit. Washington, DC.

National Park Service. n.d. "First to Serve." Last updated November 21, 2015. https://www.nps.gov/fosc/learn/historyculture/firsttoserve.htm.

Nelson, Peter B., Alexander Oberg, and Lise Nelson. 2010. "Rural Gentrification and Linked Migration in the United States." *Journal of Rural Studies* 26 (4): 343–52.

Neptune, Harvey. 2007. *Caliban and the Yankees: Trinidad and the United States Occupation*. Chapel Hill: University of North Carolina Press.

Nieves, Angel. 2008. "Introduction: Cultural Landscapes of Resistance and Self-Definition for the Race: Interdisciplinary Approaches to a Socio-Spatial Race History." In *We Shall Independent Be: African American Place-Making and the Struggle to Claim Space in the United States*, edited by Angel Nieves and Leslie Alexander, 1–22. Boulder: University Press of Colorado.

O'Dell, Larry. 2004. "All-Black Towns." In *Encyclopedia of the Great Plains*, edited by David J. Wishart, 9–10. Lincoln: University of Nebraska Press.

———. n.d. "All-Black Towns." *Encyclopedia of Oklahoma History and Culture*. Accessed May 27, 2015. https://www.okhistory.org/publications/enc/entry.php?entry=AL009.

———. n.d. "Boley," *Encyclopedia of Oklahoma History and Culture*. Accessed May 27, 2015. https://www.okhistory.org/publications/enc/entry.php?entry=BO008.

———. n.d. "Lima." *Encyclopedia of Oklahoma History and Culture*. Accessed October 20, 2015. https://www.okhistory.org/publications/enc.php?entry=LI003.

———. n.d. "Taft." *Encyclopedia of Oklahoma History and Culture*. Accessed October 20, 2015. https://www.okhistory.org/publications/enc/entry.php?entry=TA001.

Oklahoma Commission. 2001. *Tulsa Race Riot: A Report by the Oklahoma Commission to Study the Tulsa Race Riot of 1921*. February 28. http://www.okhistory.org/research/forms/freport.pdf.

Oklahoma Department of Corrections. 2002. *Report: Oklahoma Department of Corrections History: The 20th Century*. Oklahoma City, OK.

Oklahoma Historical Society. 1991. *Battlefield Protection Study: Honey Springs Battlefield Park, Oklahoma*. Prepared in cooperation with the American Battlefield Protection Program, U.S. Department of Interior. October 3, revised March 24, 1992. https://irma.nps.gov/DataStore/DownloadFile/487179.

———. n.d. "Oklahoma History Center." Accessed June 28, 2018. http://www.okhistory.org/historycenter/.

Painter, Nell. 1992. *Exodusters: Black Migration to Kansas after Reconstruction*. New York: Norton.

Patillo-McCoy, Mary. 1999. *Black Picket Fences. Privilege and Peril among the Black Middle Class*. Chicago: University of Chicago Press.

Perez, Gina. 2004. *The Near Northwest Side Story: Migration, Displacement and Puerto Rican Families*. Berkeley: University of California Press.

Phillips, Martin. 2010. "Counterurbanisation and Rural Gentrification: An Exploration of the Terms." *Population, Space and Place* 16: 539–58.

Pierre, Jemima. 2012. *The Predicament of Blackness: Postcolonial Ghana and the Politics of Race*. Chicago: University of Chicago Press.

Polanco, Mieka Brand. 2014. *Historically Black: Imagining Community in a Black Historic District*. New York: NYU Press.

Prince, Sabiyha. 2014. *African Americans and Gentrification in Washington, D.C.: Race, Class and Social Justice in the Nation's Capital*. Surrey, UK: Ashgate.

Purifoy, Danielle. 2018a. "The Water Next Time?" *Scalawag Magazine*. October 10. https://www.scalawagmagazine.org/2018/10/princeville-flooding/.

———. 2018b. "When Anti-Blackness Comes to Town." *Scalawag Magazine*. July 18.

"Quake Rattles the Town of Boley." 2013. ABC KOCONews 5, September 15. https://www.koco.com/article/quake-ratles-the-town-of-boley/3803528.

Ralph, Laurence. 2014. *Renegade Dreams: Living through Injury in Gangland Chicago*. Chicago: University of Chicago Press.

Raymond, Ken. 2012. "Endangered Black History: Past and Present Collide in Deep Deuce, Oklahoma History Center, and More." NewsOK.com. Accessed June 8, 2018. http://ndepth.newsok.com/Black-history.

Regis, Helen. 1999. "Second Lines, Minstrelsy, and the Contested Landscapes of New Orleans Afro-Creole Festivals." *Cultural Anthropology* 14 (4): 472–504.

Richards, Sandra L. 2005. "What Is to Be Remembered? Tourism to Ghana's Slave Castle-Dungeons." *Theatre Journal* 57 (4): 617–37.

Roberts, Neil. 2015. *Freedom as Marronage*. Chicago: University of Chicago Press.

Robinson, Cedric. 1983. *Black Marxism: The Making of the Black Radical Tradition*. London: Zed Books.

Robinson, Judy Gibbs. 2004. "Census Reveals Oklahoma's Deep German Roots." NewsOK.com. July 18. https://newsok.com/article/2859336/census-reveals-oklahomas-deep-german-roots.

Rodman, Margaret. 1992. "Empowering Place: Multilocality and Multivocality. *American Anthropologist* 94 (3): 640–56.

Rohrs, Richard C. 1980. "Germans." *Encyclopedia of Oklahoma History and Culture*. Accessed June 25, 2018. www.okhistory.org.

Rose, Harold. 1965. "The All-Negro Town: Its Evolution and Function." *Geographical Review* 55 (3): 362–81.

Sanchez, Juan. 2017. "Wagoner Judge Gives Tullahassee Additional Days to Pay Off Water Bill." ABC Tulsa. June 24. https://ktul.com/archive/dispute-continues-in-porter-tullahassee-over-unpaid-water-bill.

Sandoval, Denise M. 2013. "The Politics of Low and Slow/Bajito y Suavecito: Black and Chicano Lowriders in Los Angeles, from the 1960s through the 1970s." In

Black and Brown Los Angeles: Beyond Conflict and Cooperation, edited by Josh Kun and Laura Pulido, 176–202. Berkeley: University of California Press.

Schrift, Melissa. 2004. "The Angola Prison Rodeo: Inmate Cowboys and Institutional Tourism." *Ethnology* 43 (4): 331–44.

Sentencing Project. 2004. *Prison Privatization and the Use of Incarceration*. Washington, DC. Originally published 2002. https://www.prisonlegalnews.org/media/publications/the_sentencing_project_prison_privatization_and_use_of_incarceration_2000.pdf.

Sherman, Jennifer. 2009. *Those Who Work, Those Who Don't: Poverty, Morality, and Family in Rural America*. Minneapolis: University of Minnesota Press.

Simmons, Matt. 2013. "Punishment and Profits: A Brief History of Private Prisons in Oklahoma." Oklahoma Policy Institute. July 14. Updated October 5, 2016. http://okpolicy.org/punishment-and-profits-a-brief-history-of-private-prisons-in-oklahoma.

Slocum, Karla. 2017. "Caribbean Free Villages: Toward an Anthropology of Blackness, Place and Freedom." *American Ethnologist* 44 (3): 425–34.

Spurgeon, Ian Michael. 2014. *Soldiers in the Army of Freedom: The 1st Kansas Colored, the Civil War's First African American Combat Unit*. Norman: University of Oklahoma Press.

Stack, Carol. 1996. *Call to Home: African Americans Reclaim the Rural South*. New York: Basic Books.

Stillman, Peter G., and Adelaide H. Villmoare. 2010. "Democracy Despite Government: African American Parading and Democratic Theory." *New Political Science* 32 (4): 485–99.

Strain, Christopher. 2004. "Soul City, North Carolina: Black Power, Utopia and the African American Dream." *Journal of African American History* 89 (1): 57–74.

Stuckey, Melissa. 2018. "The Boley Carnival: A Juneteenth Like No Other." *The New Territory* 5: 4–9.

Stuckey, Melissa Nicole. 2009. "All Men Up: Race, Rights, and Power in the All-Black Town of Boley, Oklahoma, 1903–1939." PhD diss., Yale University.

Sturm, Circe. 2002. *Blood Politics: Race, Culture, and Identity in the Cherokee Nation of Oklahoma*. Berkeley: University of California Press.

———. 2014. "Race, Sovereignty, and Civil Rights: Understanding the Cherokee Freedmen Controversy." *Cultural Anthropology* 29 (3): 575–98. https://doi.org/10.14506/ca29.3.07.

Taylor, Erica. 2012. "Little Known Black History Fact: Boley, Oklahoma." BlackAmericaWeb. https://blackamericaweb.com/2012/10/30/little-known-black-history-fact-boley-oklahoma/.

Taylor, Quintard. 1998. *In Search of the Racial Frontier: African Americans in the American West, 1528–1990*. New York: Norton.

———. 2006. "Black Towns." In *Encyclopedia of African American History and Culture*, edited by Colin Palmer, 281–83. Detroit: Macmillan.

Thiede, Brian, and Tim Slack. 2017. "The Old versus the New Economies and Their Impacts." In *Rural Poverty in the United States*, edited by Ann R. Tickamyer,

Jennifer Sherman, and Jennifer Warlick, 231–49. New York: Columbia University Press.

Thomas, Deborah. 2004. *Modern Blackness: Nationalism, Globalization, and the Politics of Culture in Jamaica*. Durham, NC: Duke University Press.

Thomas, Lynell L. 2009. "'Roots Run Deep Here': The Construction of Black New Orleans in Post-Katrina Tourism Narratives." *American Quarterly* 41: 749–68.

Tieken, Mara Casey. 2017. "There's a Big Part to Rural America That Everyone Is Ignoring." Op-ed, *Washington Post*. March 24.

Trouillot, Michel-Rolph. 1990. "The Odd and the Ordinary: Haiti, the Caribbean and the World." *Cimarron: New Perspectives on the Caribbean* 2: 3–12.

———. 1997. *Silencing the Past: Power and the Production of History*. New York: Beacon.

Turner, Morris III. 1999. *America's Black Towns and Settlements: A Reference Guide*. Rohnert Park, CA: Missing Pages Productions.

Ulrich-Schad, Jessica D., and Cynthia M. Duncan. 2018. "People and Places Left Behind: Work, Culture and Politics in the Rural United States." *Journal of Peasant Studies* 45 (1): 59–79.

U.S. Census Bureau. 2000. "Profile of General Demographic Characteristics: 2000." Generated using American Factfinder, December 28, 2018. factfinder.census.gov.

———. 2006–2010. "American Community Survey." Generated using American Factfinder, December 5, 2018. factfinder.census.gov.

———. 2010. "Race and Hispanic or Latino Origin File." Generated using American Factfinder, December 5, 2018. factfinder.census.gov.

———. 2013–2017. "American Community Survey." Generated by American Factfinder, December 29, 2018. factfinder.census.gov.

U.S. Department of Labor, Office of Policy Planning and Research. 1965. *The Negro Family: The Case for National Action*. Washington, DC: U.S. Department of Labor. https://www.dol.gov/general/aboutdol/history/webid-moynihan.

Van Sertima, Ivan. 1976. *They Came before Columbus: The African Presence in Ancient America*. New York: Random House.

Vargas, Joao. 2006. *Catching Hell in the City of Angels*. Minneapolis: University of Minnesota Press.

Waits, Wallace, Jr. n.d. "Muskogee." *Encyclopedia of Oklahoma History and Culture*. Accessed December 30, 2018. https://www.okhistory.org/publications/enc .php?entry=MU018.

Walker, Vanessa Siddle. 1996. *Their Highest Potential: An African American School Community in the Segregated South*. Chapel Hill: University of North Carolina Press.

Washington, Booker T. 1908. "Boley: A Negro Town in the West." *The Outlook* 88: 28–81.

Wiese, Andrew. 1993. "Places of Our Own: Suburban Black Towns before 1960." *Journal of Urban History* 19: 30–54.

Wilkins, Langston Collins. 2016. "Screwston, TX: The Impact of Space, Place, and Cultural Identity on Music Making in Houston's Hip Hop Scene." PhD diss., Indiana University, Bloomington.

Williams, Bianca C. 2018. *The Pursuit of Happiness: Black Women, Diasporic Dreams, and the Politics of Emotional Transnationalism*. Durham, NC: Duke University Press.

Wilson, William Julius, Jr. 1978. *The Declining Significance of Race*. Chicago: University of Chicago Press.

———. 1987. *The Truly Disadvantaged: The Inner City, the Underclass, and Public Policy*. Chicago: University of Chicago Press.

Woods, Clyde. 1998. *Development Arrested: The Blues and Plantation Power in the Mississippi Delta*. Brooklyn, NY: Verso Books.

Woods, Michael. 2007. "Engaging the Global Countryside: Globalization, Hybridity and the Reconstitution of Rural Place." *Progress in Human Geography* 31 (4): 485–507.

Woodson, Carter Godwin. 1930. *The Rural Negro*. Washington, DC: Association for the Study of Negro Life and History.

Index

Note: Information in figures and tables is indicated by page numbers in *italics*.

Adichie, Chimamanda Ngozi, 38–39
African Americans, 142n12; Black
   identity and, 17; in census, 13; in Civil
   War, 45, 63, 147n35; in diasporic
   encounters, 142n12; family reunions
   among, 124; Freedmen and, 3–4; in
   Great Migration, 3, 141n7; lowrider
   culture among, 117; and police
   brutality, 7; as tourists, 43, 51. *See also
   entries at* Black; Native Blacks
African American Trails, 59–61, 68, 82
Alaraf organization, 115
All-Black Towns, 1
All-Negro Societies, ix
American Indian, 16–17. *See also* Native
   Americans
Anadarko, Oklahoma, 138
automobiles, lowrider, *117*, 117–18, *118*,
   118–20

Barber, Kari, 137
Basso, Keith, 8
Battle of Honey Springs, 45, 61–66,
   62, 137
Bering Strait Land-Bridge Theory,
   46–47, 146n14
Black communities, 6–7, 56–61, 129–30,
   142n30
Black Heritage Society of Tulsa, 40,
   42–44
Black mobility, 11, 26–33, 118–19, 123,
   143n38, 148n13
blackness, 17, 130–31, 133–34;
   affirmation of, 11; Americanness and,
   67; and Boley Rodeo and Bar-B-Q, 115,
   119; and geographic violence, 10; and

lowrider culture, 118; parades and,
   120; place and, 6; in tours, 42, 51–61
Black sense of place, 8–11, 131–32,
   143n38
Black spatial imaginary, 12, 131–33
Black towns, 13–18; appeal of, to
   tourists, 67–68; defined, 131;
   demographics of, 13–14, 138, 147n1,
   148n20; fragility of, 132–33; as ghost
   towns, 69; historical significance of,
   41, 43–44, 145n2; as imagined places,
   11–12; investment in, 86–96, *91*;
   precarity of, 133, 136–37; racial
   demographics of, 147n1; recruiters
   for, 4–5; senses of place of, 6–13;
   whitening of, 14, 90–95, 138
Black Towns, The (Crockett), 27
"Black Wall Streets," 9, 54
blood quantum, 146n28
Blue, Rob, 88
Boley, Oklahoma, x, 1, 15, *28*, 70, 134,
   135; in 2016 presidential election, 138;
   and Booker T. Washington, 26–27;
   businesses in, 73–74; census data and
   institutions in, 14; earthquakes in,
   137; fracking in, 137; motto of, 29; in
   NewsOk.com series, 137; prison in,
   96, 98–99, *99*, 99–100, 102, 149n34;
   and respectability, 27–28; schools in,
   33–34, *135*; tours of, 44; Town Council
   (circa 1907–1910), *28*; women in
   leadership of, 80–81
Boley Carnival, 110
Boley Elementary School, *135*
Boley Rodeo and Bar-B-Q, 109–21, *111*,
   113, *116–18*

Boley State School for Incorrigible Negro Boys, 98
Bronzeville (Chicago), 10
buffalo soldiers, 45, 63
businesses, 26–31, 73–81, 74

Call to Home (Stack), 106
Canada, 146n16
cars, lowrider, *117*, 117–18, *118*, 118–20
Carson, Oklahoma (pseudonym), 71
census, 6, 13–14, 16, 69, 138, 147n1, 148n20
Cha-Jua, Sundiata, 131
Cherokee Freedmen, 55–56
Cherokee Nation, 56, 147n28
Chester, Simon, 81–82, 84–86, 105
Chicago, Illinois, 9, 91
Chocolate Cities (Hunter and Robinson), 10
Civil War, 45, 61–66, 62, 147n35
class distinctions, 148n13
Clinton, Hillary, 138
Coltrane Group, 137
Coyle, Oklahoma, ix–x
Creek Nation, 14, 48–49
Crockett, Norman L., 27, 145nn10–11
Cromwell School, 36–38

Davis, Leila Foley, 149n34
Dawes Act, 46, 56
Dawes Commission, 56
Dawes Rolls, 146n28
Deep North Tulsa, 52
Deloria, Vine, 47
diasporic encounters, 3, 51, 142n12
Dr. Eddie Warrior Correctional Center, 98, 99, 100
Dunlap, Priscilla, 36–38, 103
Durham, North Carolina, 9, 42
Dusk 'til Dawn Blues Festival, 109, 149n5

earthquakes, 136–37
Eason, John, 96–97
Eatonville, Florida, 82, 144n7
Emancipation, 3

Feld, Steven, 8
First Kansas Colored Infantry, 63, 65, 147n35
"Five Civilized Tribes," 49–50
Fort Coffee, Oklahoma, 138
Fort Gibson Historic Site, 45, 63
fracking, 136–37
fragility, 132–33
Franklin, John Hope, 44, 66
Freedmen, 3–4, 46–48, 55–56, 142n12, 147n28
Freeland, Oklahoma (pseudonym), 14, 70, 78–80, 89–90, *91*, 108
Freeman, Lance, 147n7

gender, 29, 148n12
gentrification, 10, 85, 89, 147n7
geographic violence, 10
German migration, 145n17
Great Depression, 5, 19
Great Migration, 3, 141n7
Green Valley, Oklahoma (pseudonym), 15, 32, 40, 45, 52, 61
Greenwood (Tulsa neighborhood), 25, 42, 54–56
Grinde, Donald A., Jr., 142n12
Guthrie, Oklahoma, x, 13, 15, 141n1

Haiti, 67–68, 144n6
Harlem, 10
Harlemworld (Jackson), 43
heritage tourism, 41–44, 61, 63, 67–68, 137
Hill, Letchen, *135*
Hill, Mozell C., 4, 30, 87, 119, 128
historical significance, 41, 43–44, 145n2
Holsey, Bayo, 19–20
Honey Springs Battlefield, 45, 61–66, 62, 137
Humphrey, Charles A., 34
Hunter, Marcus, 8, 10
Hurston, Zora Neale, 82. *See also* Eatonville, Florida

Industrial Institute for the Deaf, Blind, and Orphans of the Colored Race, 98, 102–4
inequality: and Black sense of place, 8; diversification and, 93; prisons and, 99; spatial, 8–11, 143n38; structural, 17
infrastructure, 44, 69–72, 86, 97, 114, 132–33, 136–37
investment, 86–96, 91

Jackson, John L., 43
Jefferson, Thomas, 126
Jess Dunn Correctional Center, 98, 99, 100, 101
Jewel, Oklahoma (pseudonym), 15, 91
Jim Crow, 21
John H. Lilley Correctional Center, 98, 99, 100
John Hope Franklin Center for Reconciliation, 54
Jones, Bob, 83–84
Joyner, Tom, 28

Kerner Report, 142n30
Key, Keegan-Michael, 7–8
Key and Peele, 7
Kidder, Oklahoma (pseudonym), 15, 24
King, Martin Luther, Jr., 126–27
King's Prairie, Oklahoma (pseudonym), 15, 90, 91
Ku Klux Klan, 21, 59–61
Kroeker, Marvin, 150n10

Lacy, Karyn, 6–7
Langston, Oklahoma, ix, x, 15, 74, 134; in 2016 presidential election, 138; census data and institutions in, 14; McCabe and, 4; in NewsOk.com series, 137; in old film footage, 57; parades in, 120; tours of, 44–45
Langston University, 57
Lima, Oklahoma, 34–36
Lipsitz, George, 12
lowriders, 117, 117–18, 118, 118–20

Mandela, Nelson, 42
maroon villages, 9
Massey, Doreen, 8, 143n38
McAuley, William, 146n19
McCabe, Edwin P., 4
McKittrick, Katherine, 8, 10, 13, 143n38
Mennonites, 115, 150n10
Mexico, 146n14, 150n10
Minner, DC, 44, 66, 149n5
Minner, Selby, 149n5
mobility, Black, 11, 26–31, 33, 118–19, 123, 143n38, 148n13
Modern Blackness (Thomas), 119
Morrison, Toni, 11
Mound Bayou, Mississippi, 144n7
mounds, 47–48
Moynihan, Daniel, 72
Moynihan Report, 72
Muskogee, Oklahoma, 13, 15–16, 57

National Museum of African American History and Culture (NMAAHC), 49, 137
Native Americans, 14, 55–56, 65, 141n8. *See also* American Indian; Creek Nation; Perryman family
Native Blacks, 46–50, 146n19, 147n28
Native towns, 46
Negrotown (sketch), 7–8, 11
neoliberal economy, 11, 16, 71, 96, 144n72
"New Great Migration," 106–7
New Orleans, Louisiana, 12, 42, 120
Newtown, Oklahoma (pseudonym), 14, 23–24, 108; development in, 69–70; revitalization of, 107; schools in, 34; Whites in, 89; women in, 148n12
Newtown Will Rise Again, 107
North Tulsa, 48, 50–56

OCBM. *See* Oklahoma Council of Black Mayors (OCBM)
Okemah, Oklahoma, 111, 115
Oklahoma Children's Center 103

Oklahoma City, Oklahoma, 13–16,
40–41, 45, 57, 76–77, *116*, 141n1
Oklahoma City bombing (1995),
40–41
Oklahoma Council of Black Mayors
(OCBM), 15
Oklahoma Historical Society, 29
Oklahoma History Center, 19–21, *20*,
40, 144n6
Oklahoma State Penitentiary, 97
Oklahoma State Reformatory, 97
Oklahoma Territory, 141n8
Okmulgee, Oklahoma, 59, 120
Olmecs, 146n14

Paden, Oklahoma, 111
parades, 120
Paradise (Morrison), 11
Peele, Jordan, 7–8
Perryman, Legus C., 50
Perryman, Lewis, 49
Perryman family, 48–50, 53
Pineway, Oklahoma (pseudonym), 15,
36, 94
Polanco, Mieka, 144n6, 145n2
police, 7, 121
Porter, E. Melvin, 149n34
Porter, Oklahoma, 136
power geometry, 143n38
precarity, 133, 136–37
prison industrial complex, 10
prisons, as development, 96–104, *99*,
101, 149n32
Promise, Oklahoma (pseudonym),
14–15, 24–25, 36–37, 108, 121–25;
development in, 69; property
investment in, 93–95; racism and,
58–61; schools in, 34, 37; Whites in,
89; women in, 148n12

Race Attitude Test, 128
racialization, 10, 60, 88, 117, 133
racism: and African American Trails, 61;
and Black communities, 58–61; and
Black migration, 3; Black towns as

bastions from, x, 1; and sense of
place, 6; structural, 38
Ralph, Laurence, 72
Ray, Raymond, 95
recruiters, 4–5
Redbird, Oklahoma, 52
Red Earth, White Lies (Deloria), 47
Red Hats (women's organization), 115
redistricting, 10
redlining, 10
Rentiesville, Oklahoma, 15; business
in, 73; Dusk 'til Dawn Blues Festival
in, 109, 149n5; Honey Springs
Battlefield and, 65–66, 137; Minner
and, 66, 149n5; North Tulsa and, 52;
tours of, 44–45
respectability, 26–31, 80, 118–20
reunions, 37–38, 123–24
"riots" (1921 Greenwood), 54–55
Robben Island (South Africa), 42
Roberts, Neil, 9
Robinson, Zandria, 8, 10
rodeo parade, 109–121, *111*, *113*, *116–18*
Rose, Harold, 131
Rosenwald, Julius, 34
runaway slaves, 9
rural America, 11, 16, 69, 73, 138–39

sanctuaries, 9
schools, 31–38, *35*, *135*
Schrift, Melissa, 149n36
sense of place, 6–13, 131–32, 143n38
sharecropping, 24–25
Simms, Gina, 95
Singleton, Benjamin "Pap," 4
slaves, runaway, 9
Soul City, North Carolina, 9
South Africa, 42
spatial imaginary: Black, 12, 131–33
spatial inequality, 8–11, 143n38
spatial racialization, 133
spatial violence, 10–11, 134
Stack, Carol, 16, 106
State Blacks, 46
State towns, 46

Struggle and Hope (film), 137
Stuckey, Melissa, 110
Sturm, Circe, 56
Suffrage Act, 60
Summit, Oklahoma, 52
Sweethearts of the Prison Rodeo (film),
  100–101, 149n36

Taft, Oklahoma, 15, 29, *101*; in 2016 presi-
  dential election, 138; census data and
  institutions in, 14; Deaf, Blind, and
  Orphan institute in, 102–4; North Tulsa
  and, 52; parade in, 120; prison in, 96,
  98–99, *99*, 99–101, 149n34; tours of, 44
Tatums, Oklahoma, 20
Taylor, Quintard, 142n12
Tennessee Self-Concept Scale, 127
They Came before Columbus (Van
  Sertima), 47
Thomas, Deborah A., 119
Thomas, Lynell, 42
Tieken, Mara Casey, 139
Tom Joyner Radio, 28
tourism, 42–43, 51, 67–68, 137. *See also*
  heritage tourism
trauma, 38–39
Trouillot, Michel-Rolph, 67–68, 144n6
Trump, Donald, 138–39
Tullahassee, Oklahoma, 52, 136
Tulsa, Oklahoma, 9, 13, 42, 45–56. *See
  also* North Tulsa
Turner, John, 94–95

urban renewal, 10
utopianism, 4

Van Sertima, Ivan, 47, 146n14
violence: geographic, 10; spatial,
  10, 134

Walker, Ben, 40, 52
Walker, Madam C. J., 57
Walker, Vanessa Siddle, 33
Washington, Booker T., 26–27, 30, 110,
  144n7
water, 136
Weewoka, Oklahoma, 115
white investments, 86–96, *91*
whitening, 14, 90–95, 138
Whites: in business, 87–88; in economy,
  88–89; increase in population of,
  138; in periphery of Black towns,
  90–92; as property investors,
  93–95
Wiese, Andrew, 131
Wrightsville, Oklahoma (pseudonym),
  14–15, 22–23, 81–86, 92–93, 102, 108,
  126–29; business in, 30–31, 74–78,
  148n12; development in, 69–71, 105;
  prison in, 96; schools in, 31–33,
  36–37; Whites in, 89; women in,
  148n12
Wrightsville Vocational School, 35–36

Yamassee, 49

www.ingramcontent.com/pod-product-compliance
Lightning Source LLC
Chambersburg PA
CBHW030333270326
41926CB00010B/1601